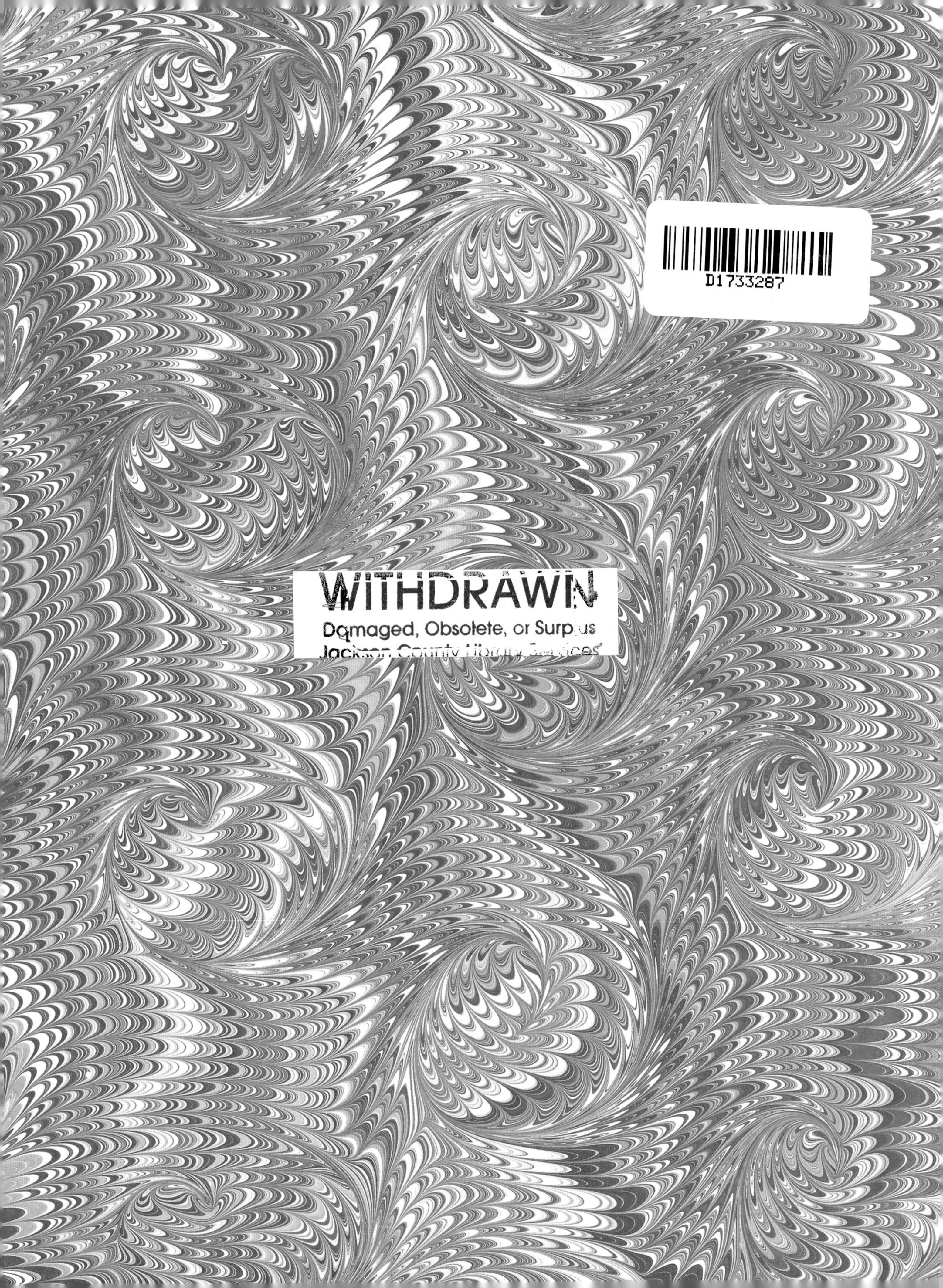
D1733287
WITHDRAWN
Damaged, Obsolete, or Surplus
Jackson County Library Services

United States Army Shoulder Patches and Related Insignia

By the Author

United States Army Shoulder Patches and Related Insignia From World War I to Korea
1st Division to 40th Division

United States Army Shoulder Patches and Related Insignia From World War I to Korea
41st Division to 106th Division

United States Army Shoulder Patches and Related Insignia

From World War I to Korea

41st Division to 106th Division

William Keller
& Kurt Keller

Schiffer Military History
Atglen, PA

Acknowledgments

My sincerest gratitude goes out to all that helped and made the production of this volume possible. Namely Dan Alloggio, Kurt H. Andariese, David S. Angle, Peter M. Bennethum, Gary Castellino, Rocco Collura, David Fisher, John Foley, Mike Furey, Scott Glemby, Bob Ford, Richard T. Graney, Daniel Griffin, Kurt Keller, James E. Mullin, Bruce J. Pitre Jr., Gus Radle, James F. Rudy, Garth Thompson, Charles Van Der Eems, and John B. Wright. Without any of whom this book would not have been as complete or accurate. I wish to commend them for their hospitality and cooperation. It was a unique privilege to be invited to view their collections and photograph the best each had to offer. Without exception, each visit was a wonderful learning experience. Their dedication not just to collecting but the preservation of history made this project a joy to work on and the photographs contained within speak volumes to the lifetime commitment it has been for many of them. I'm especially grateful to the individuals who graciously provided me with identification for some of the more unusual pieces. One last note, I would like to especially thank those brave souls who mailed me photos and patches to photograph.

To all the soldiers who served, both remembered and forgotten.

Book design by Robert Biondi.
Principal photography by Kurt Keller; additional photography by William Keller.
Dust jacket photo by Robert Biondi.

Library of Congress Catalog Number: 2001093488.

Printed in China.
ISBN: 0-7643-1502-1

We are always looking for people to write books on new and related subjects. If you have an idea for a book, please contact us at the address below.

Published by Schiffer Publishing Ltd.
4880 Lower Valley Road
Atglen, PA 19310
Phone: (610) 593-1777
FAX: (610) 593-2002
E-mail: Schifferbk@aol.com.
Visit our web site at: www.schifferbooks.com
Please write for a free catalog.
This book may be purchased from the publisher.
Please include $3.95 postage.
Try your bookstore first.

In Europe, Schiffer books are distributed by:
Bushwood Books
6 Marksbury Ave.
Kew Gardens
Surrey TW9 4JF
England
Phone: 44 (0)208 392-8585
FAX: 44 (0)208 392-9876
E-mail: Bushwd@aol.com.
Free postage in the UK. Europe: air mail at cost.
Try your bookstore first.

Contents

Use Guide and Abbreviation Key

Use this section as a quick reference point for the manufacturing style codes listed in the captions. For ease of use, each Division will be its own chapter. Within each chapter each photo caption will contain all the information about each patch. After the patch number, the period the patch is from is listed. This is followed by the Country of origin and, if unique beyond the divisional identity, the identification of the patch and finally the construction description. All patches without a country listed, with the exception of World War I's are believed to be made in the United States. Information not covered by the introduction will be discussed in the caption when the topic is reached – see the following sample entry:

> *Fig. 8.16.* Post World War II, Germany. Bullion and felt. Translation: 8th Division, Patch 16, manufactured after World War II, made in Germany, bullion and felt construction.

Bullion = Any spun, woven or wrapped metallic thread.

CS = Chain Stitch: Two top threads attached to base material by a single pick up or backing thread. Under close examination this embroidery type resembles a chain. This technique is usually done with a hand guided embroidery machine. A hand embroidered technique also exists that resembles this stitch pattern.

DI = Distinguished Unit Insignia: Metal insignia with enameled or painted designs commonly found for regimental units. Occasionally these can be found in miniature patch form for wear on Garrison caps, lapels and shoulder straps.

ET = Embroidered on twill: Any patch where exposed twill base material is part of the design of the patch.

FE = Fully embroidered: The embroidery covers the entire surface of the patch.

Felt = Pressed woolen material that has no weave.

HE = Hand Embroidered: The design of the patch is embroidered with needle and thread by hand.

ME = Machine embroidered: The design is embroidered on material with a machine guided by a prepared pattern.

ODB = Olive Drab Border

TM = Patch is believed to be theater made but is of an unknown origin.

Wool = Wool that is a woven cloth with or without texture.

? = The possibility exists that the patch is from this period or country of origin.

Introduction

United States Army Patches, and Related Insignia from World War I to Korea - 41st Division to 106th Division is the second volume in a series of the story of the shoulder patch. This volume again brings to light the long and interesting tale of the shoulder patch through a wide array of color and sepia tone photographs. I was very pleased to be able to find such a nice balance of original insignia and original photos for the reader. This was not such an easy feat, as many of the units in this volume existed for far less time than their cousins in the first volume. As with the first volume the subject range spans the period of the Doughboys "over there" to after the Korean War, and keeping the peace in post-World War II Europe and Asia. Once again I would like to thank all those who helped in the preparation of this volume and the patience of a few who were interested enough to ask (most persistently), "when is this thing coming out?" None the less, I hope that you will find this effort as worthwhile and enjoyable as the first.

Bill Keller
July 1, 2001

United States Army
Shoulder Patches and Related Insignia

41st Division to 106th Division

Fig. 41.1. World War I. Unidentified doughboy wearing an embroidered style 41st Division patch.

Fig. 41.2. World War I. Multi-piece wool and felt applied to wool background.

Fig. 41.3. World War I. Felt on felt with an applied wool border. Many variations of the 41st Division patch can be found with this construction style.

Fig. 41.4. World War I. HE on wool with an applied wool border.

Fig. 41.5. World War I. Unidentified 41st Division doughboy wearing a patch similar to *Fig. 41.4*.

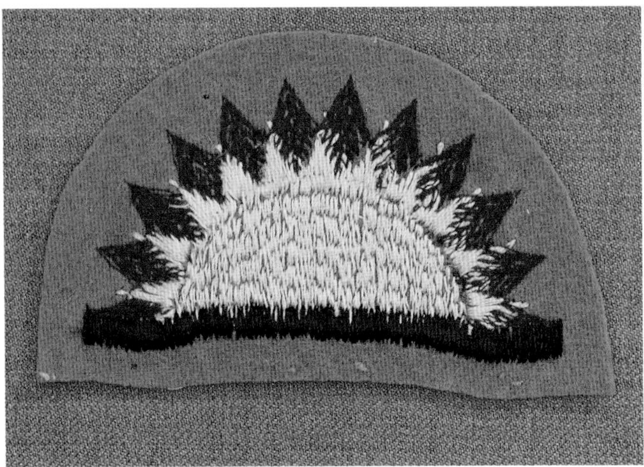

Figs. 41.6 and 41.7. World War I. ME on felt.

Fig. 41.8. World War I. ME on wool.

Fig. 41.9. World War I. CS on wool.

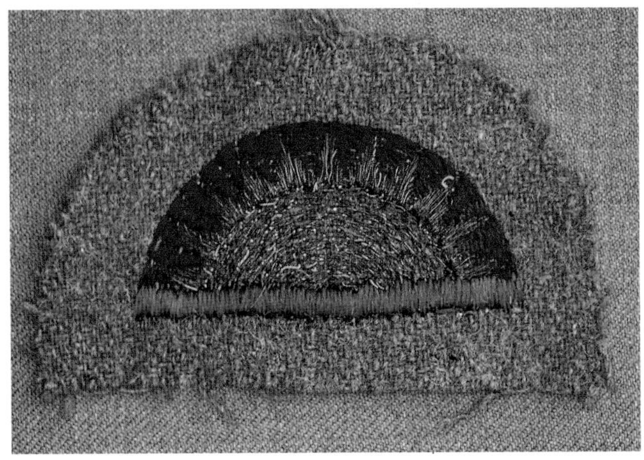

Fig. 41.10. World War I. Machine embroidered bullion on wool.

Fig. 41.11. World War I. Machine embroidered bullion on felt.

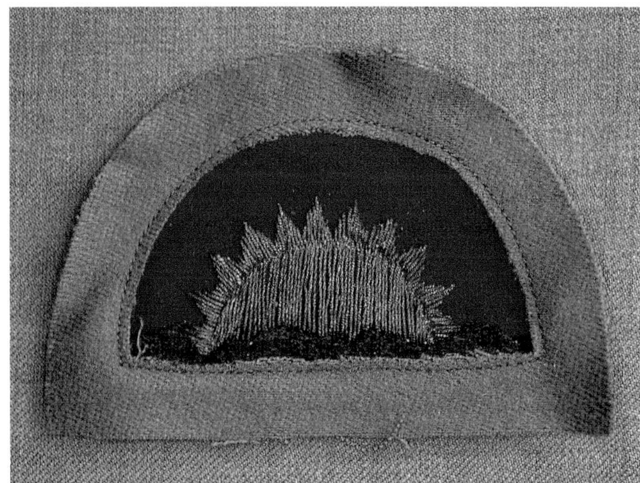

Figs. 41.12 to 41.14. Above and below left: World War I. HE bullion on wool with applied wool border.

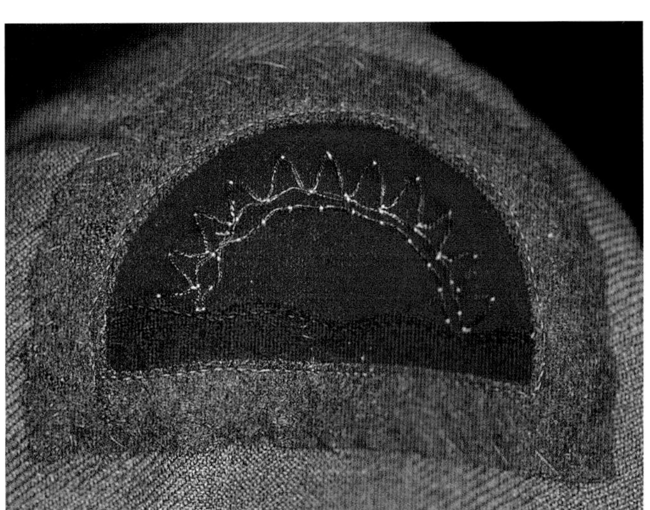

Fig. 41.15. World War I. HE bullion on wool with hand embroidered ocean and applied wool border.

Fig. 41.16. World War I. HE embroidered on textured velvet with cloth tape ocean and applied wool border.

Fig. 41.17. World War I. Bullion tape on cotton background with applied satin ribbon sun and ocean with applied wool border.

Fig. 41.18. World War I. Miniature garrison cap patch. ME on felt.

Fig. 41.19. Interwar. HE on felt.

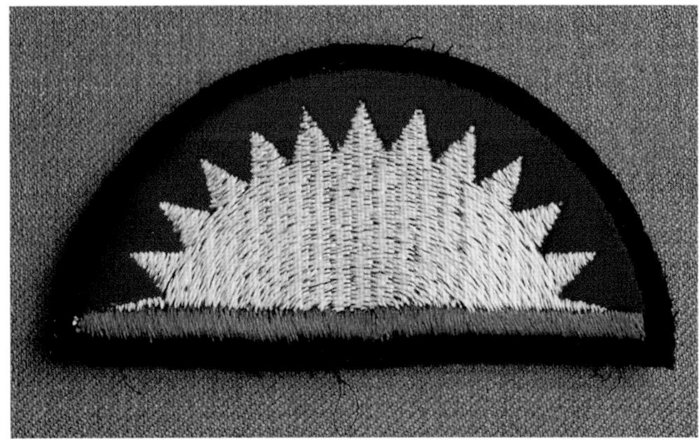

Fig. 41.20. Interwar. ME on wool.

Fig. 41.21. Interwar. ME on twill.

Fig. 41.22. Interwar. Different layers of cotton cloth glued together.

Figs. 41.23 and 41.24. World War II. FE.

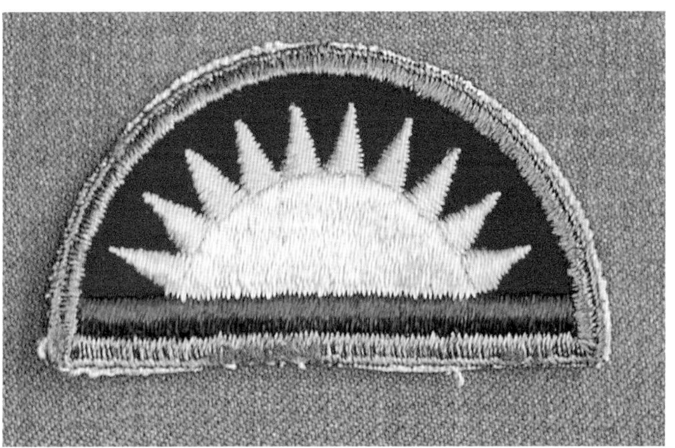

Fig. 41.25. World War II. Variation with no half rays at the ocean line. FE.

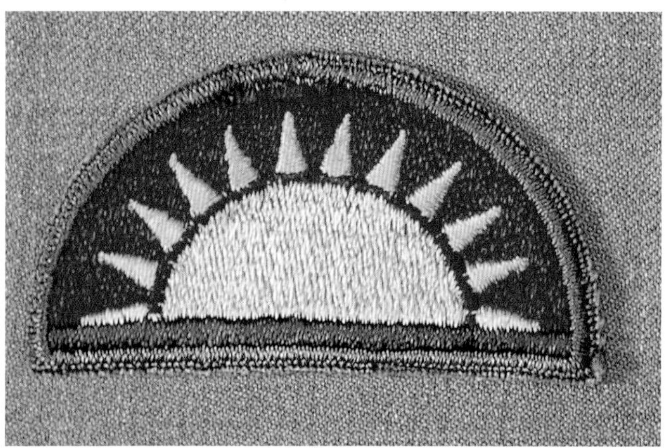

Fig. 41.26. Post World War II, Germany. FE.

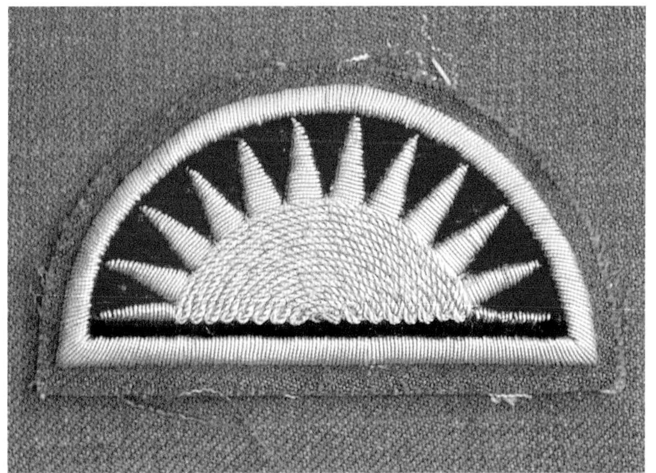

Fig. 41.27. Post World War II, Germany. Felt insert with hand embroidered cello cording on wool.

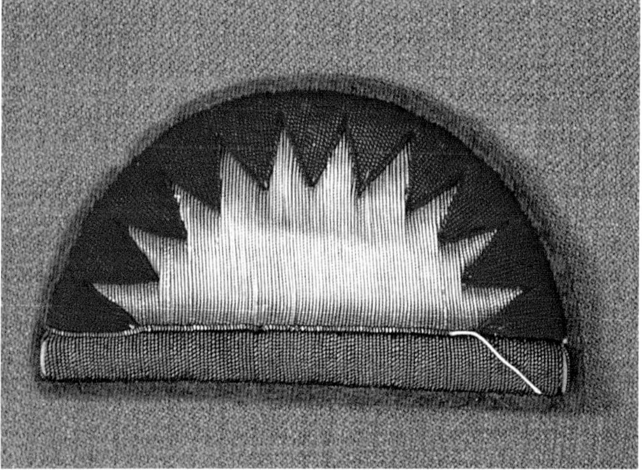

Fig. 41.28. Post World War II, Germany. HE bullion and cord on felt.

Fig. 41.29. Post World War II, Germany. Bullion and cord on felt with bullion wire twist border.

Fig. 41.30. Post World War II, Japan. Bullion on cotton cloth with HE ocean and bullion border applied to wool base.

Fig. 41.31. Post World War II, Japan. Bullion on felt with bullion border applied to felt base.

Fig. 42.1. World War I. Unidentified 42nd Division doughboy wearing a machine embroidered on felt or wool patch. Of special note is the small 42nd Division insignia on his garrison cap.

Fig. 42.2. World War I. Wool rainbow applied to a wool base.

Fig. 42.3. World War I. Felt rainbow applied to a wool base.

Fig. 42.4. World War I. Unidentified 42nd Division doughboy.

Fig. 42.5. World War I. 42nd Division medic with an applied style shoulder patch.

Fig. 42.6. World War I. All felt applied construction. Show here is one variation of rainbow lengths that can be found. During World War I sizes ranged from half rainbows (90 degrees) to a full rainbow (180 degrees).

Fig. 42.7. World War I. Applied silk construction.

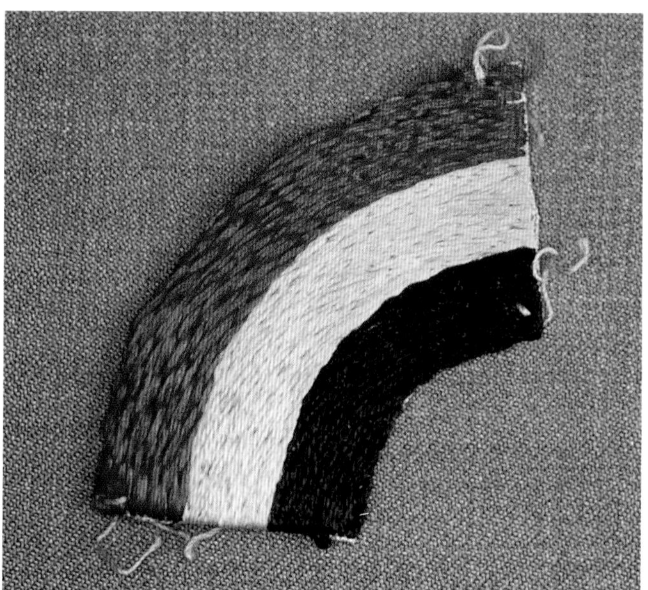

Fig. 42.8. World War I. HE silk on cotton base.

Figs. 42.9 to 42.10. Above and below: World War I. ME on felt. ***Fig. 42.10***. Private Lawrence Henritzy.

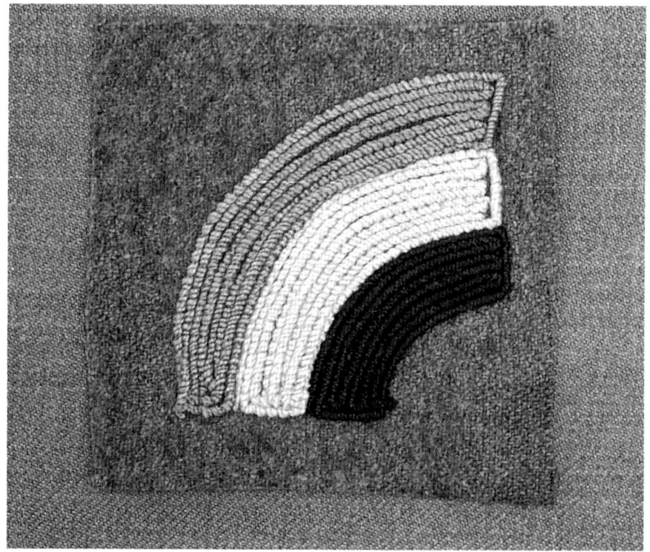

Fig. 42.11. World War I. Cotton cording applied to a wool base.

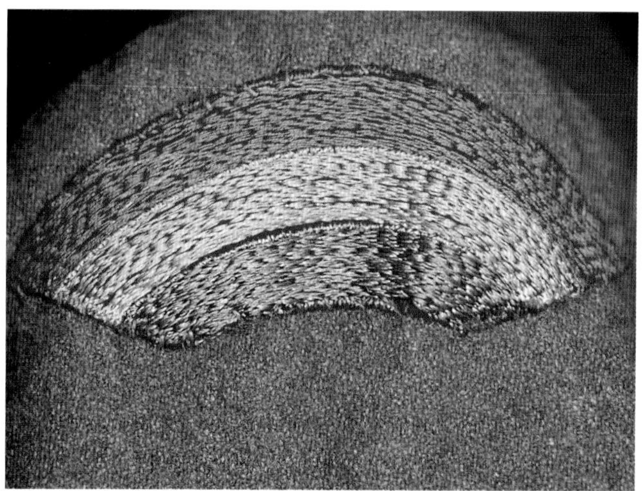

Fig. 42.12. World War I. ME on wool.

Figs. 42.13 and 42.14. Above and below: World War I. Soutache applied to a wool base.

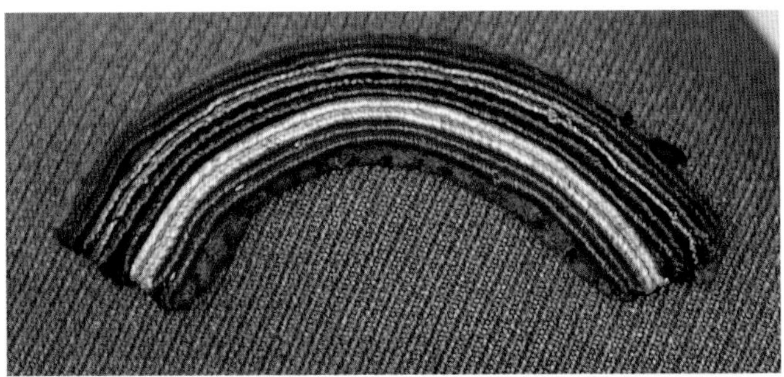

Fig. 42.15. World War I. Liberty Loan.

Fig. 42.16. World War I. Corporal Frank Brandreth, 165th Infantry Regiment. CS on wool shield.

Fig. 42.17. World War I. Corporal Brandreth's "Welcome Home" ribbon.

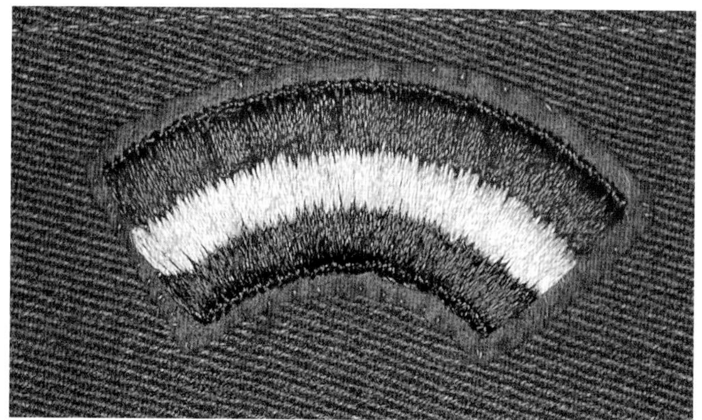

Fig. 42.18. World War I. Shoulder patch sewn to a garrison cap. ME on felt.

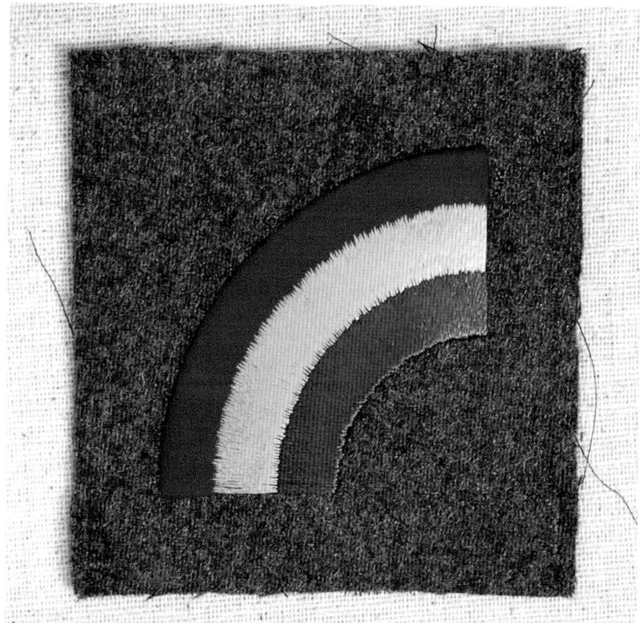

Fig. 42.19. Interwar. ME on wool.

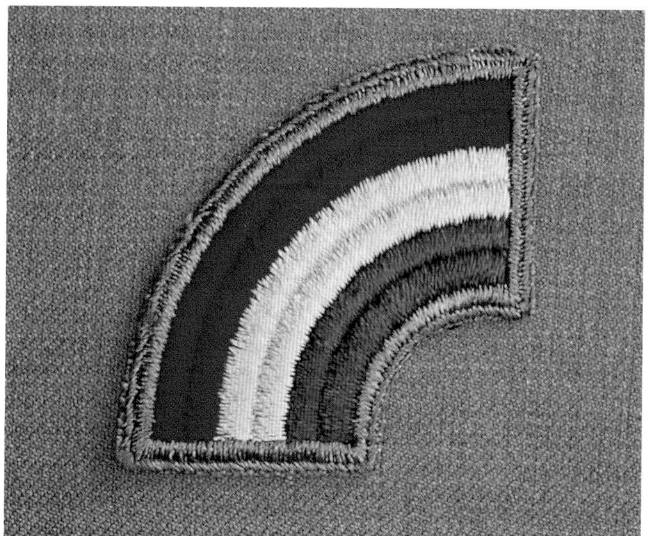

Figs. 42.20 and 42.21. Above and below: World War II. FE.

Fig. 42.22. World War II/Post World War II, TM. HE on wool.

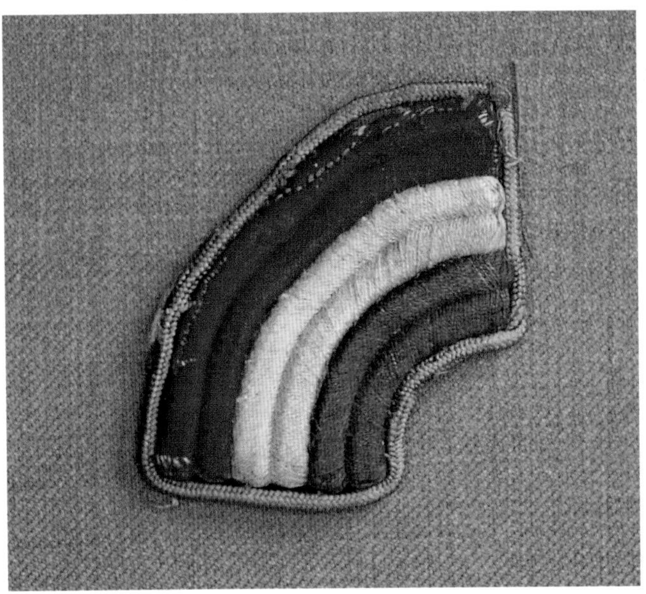

Fig. 42.23. World War II/Post World War II, TM. A very unusually constructed 42nd Division patch featuring heavy piping and a parachute cord border.

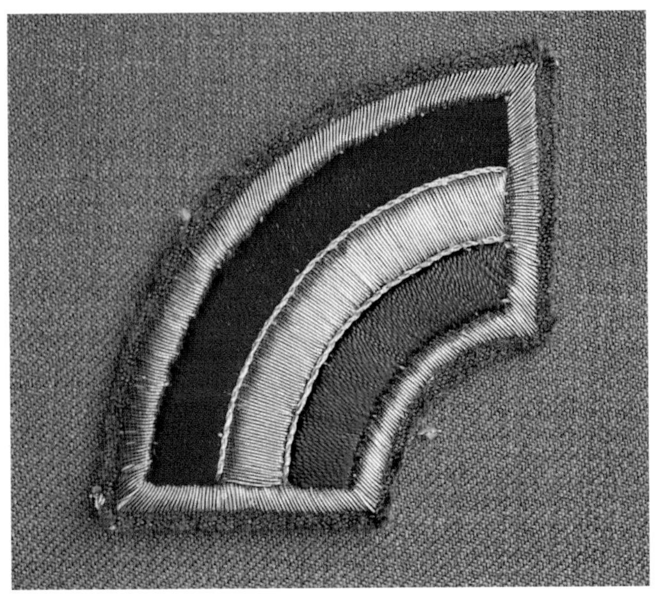

Figs. 42.24 and 42.25. Above and below: Post World War II, Germany. Two different bullion and cord 42nd Division patches. HE on wool base.

Fig. 42.26. Post World War II, Germany. HE bullion and cord on wool base patch with a HE on wool nickname tab.

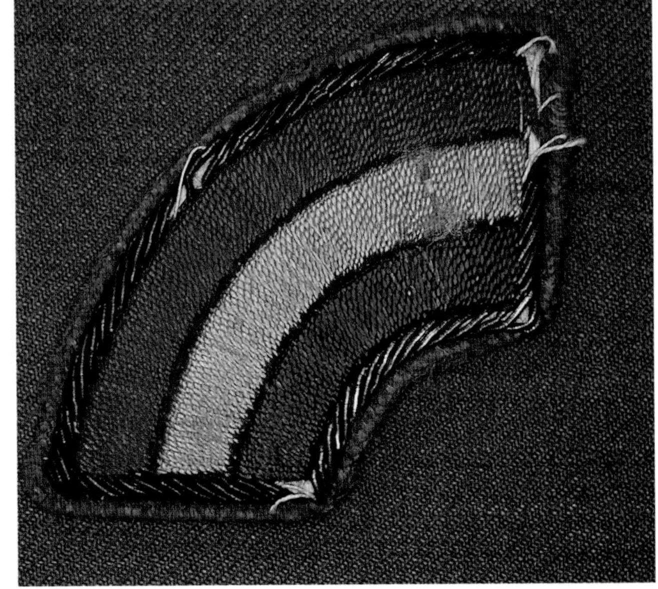

Fig. 43.1. Interwar. ME on red felt with "43" at center. Many interwar variations carry the division's numerical designation at the center of the maple leaf.

Figs. 43.2 to 43.5. Above and three below: Interwar. ME on OD felt.

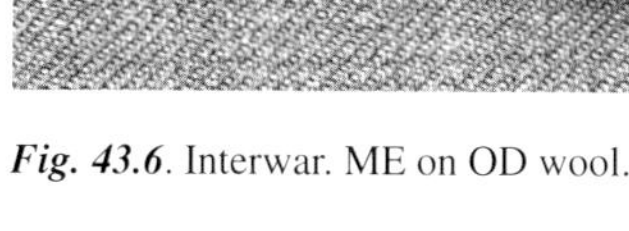

Fig. 43.6. Interwar. ME on OD wool.

Fig. 43.7. Interwar. Wide variation without "43" at center. ME on OD felt

Fig. 43.8. Interwar. HE on OD wool disk.

Figs. 43.9 and 43.10. Above and below: Interwar. Two different ME on OD wool patches.

Fig. 43.11. Interwar. ME on white felt disk.

Fig. 43.12. World War II. FE. Four different examples of U.S. made OD border 43rd Division patches. Of special note are the varying stem directions of the top two examples and the HE white detail added to the lower left example.

Fig. 43.14. World War II. FE. Unusual white border variation.

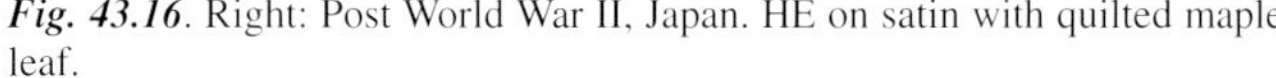

Fig. 43.16. Right: Post World War II, Japan. HE on satin with quilted maple leaf.

Fig. 43.13. World War II. FE. Side by side comparison of an OD border and a khaki border patch.

Fig. 43.15. World War II/Post World War II, Philippines. Another white border variation.

Fig. 43.17. Post World War II, Japan. Fully hand embroidered silk with a white border.

Fig. 43.18. Post World War II, Japan. Colored bullion leaf on a felt background. Also pictured a bullion on felt Presidential Unit Citation.

Fig. 43.19. World War II/Post World War II. FE. Comparison of U.S. made patches, top, and German made patches, bottom.

Fig. 43.20. Post World War II, Germany. FE. Four different examples of German made OD border patches.

Fig. 43.21. Post World War II, Germany. Woven front attached to a cotton backing.

Fig. 43.22. Post World War II, Germany. HE on felt with a bullion border applied to a khaki cotton disk.

Figs. 43.23 and 43.24. Post World War II, Germany. HE on felt with bullion details and bullion border.

Fig. 43.25. Post World War II, Germany. HE on felt patch with bullion details and border and a HE on felt with bullion border "Germany" tab.

Fig. 43.26. Post World War II, Germany. HE on felt patch with bullion details and border with a FE tab.

Fig. 43.27. Left: Post World War II, Germany. HE on satin patch and tab.

Fig. 43.28. Post World War II, Germany. Another example of a 43rd Division "Germany" tab. HE on felt with bullion border.

Fig. 44.1. Above: Interwar. Felt on felt construction.

Fig. 44.2. Above right: Interwar. Yellow wool embroidered to an OD wool background. For this example the embroidery serves to attach the two pieces of wool together.

Fig. 44.3. Interwar. ME on felt.

Figs. 44.4 and 44.5. Two at right: Interwar. ME on wool.

Fig. 44.6. Interwar. An interesting variation of a 44th Division patch. Very similar to ***Fig. 44.5*** but with the addition of a merrowed border. The merrowed edge or border process was invented in the 1930s but was little used in the making of military patches until the Army adopted its wide scale use in 1968.

Figs. 44.7 to 44.9. Above and two below: World War II. FE, ODB.

Figs. 44.10 and 44.11. World War II. FE. Two different examples of a non OD border 44th Division patch.

Fig. 44.12. Post World War II, Germany. HE on felt.

Figs. 45.1 and 45.2. Above and below: Interwar. Felt on felt. Illustrated here are two examples of the first design worn by the 45th Division. The division hailed from the southwest and took as its insignia the swastika, a Native American symbol for good luck. This design was rescinded and replaced by the Thunderbird on May 22, 1939.

Figs. 45.3 to 45.5. Three at right: Interwar. Three different examples of ME on wool "Thunderbird" 45th Division patches.

Fig. 45.6. Interwar/World War II. ME on felt.

Fig. 45.7. World War II. FE. This example features an unusual kelly green border.

Figs. 45.08 to 45.11. Above and two at top of page 34: World War II. Four different variations of a fully embroidered OD border patch.

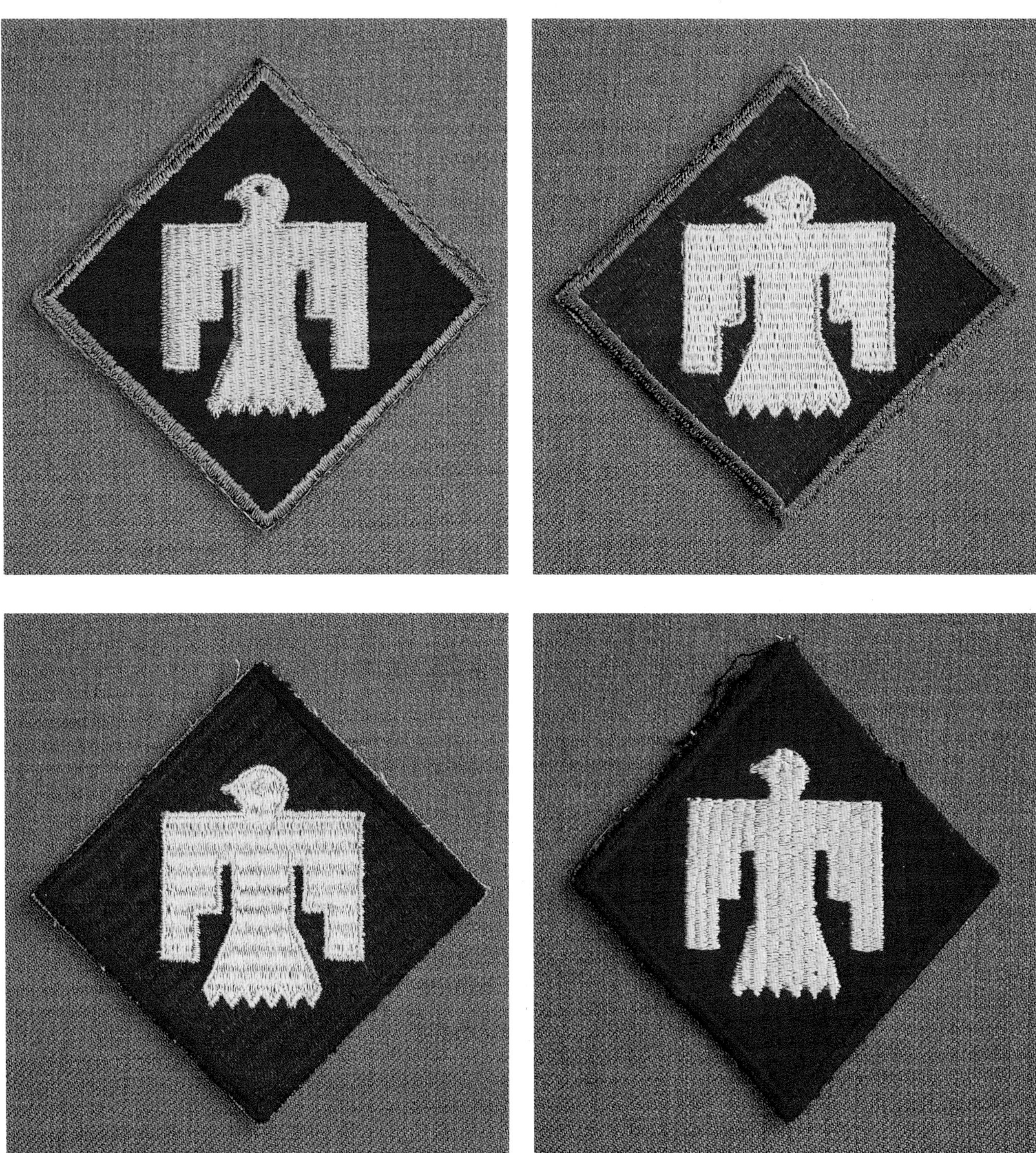

Figs. 45.12 and 45.13. World War II. FE.

Figs. 45.14 and 45.15. World War II, Italy. Front and back of an Italian made woven patch.

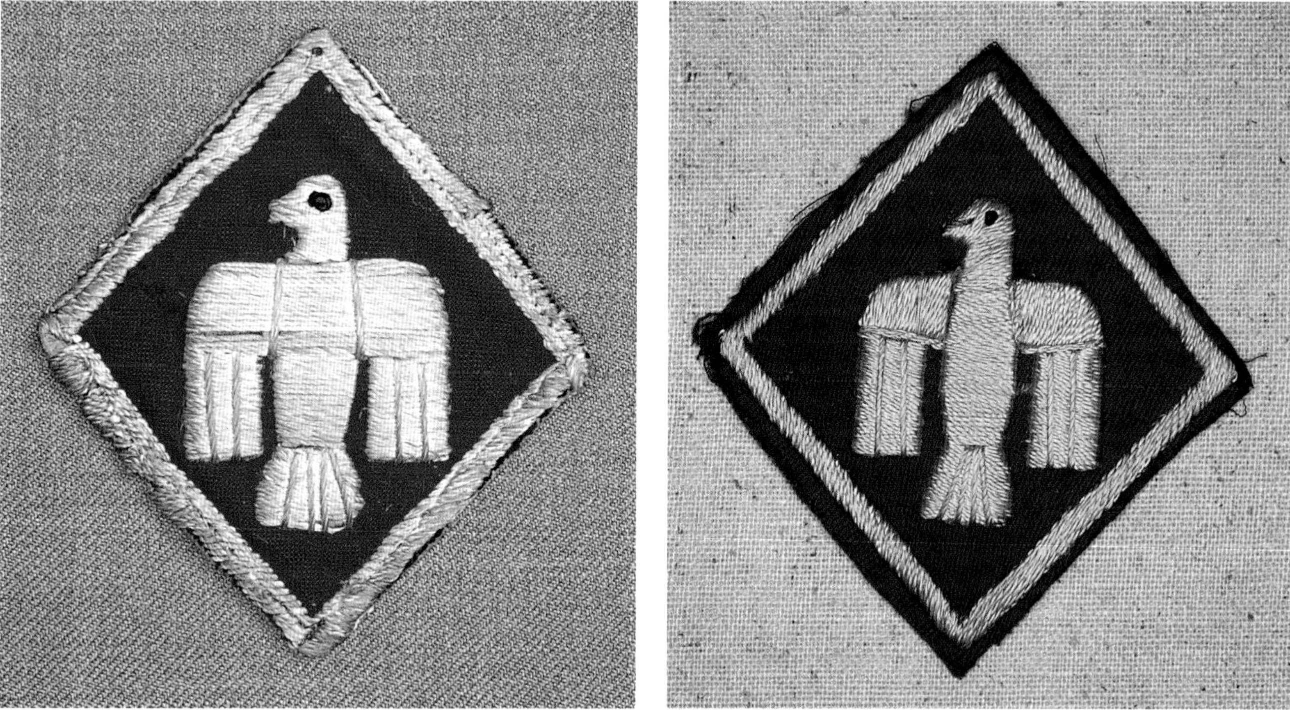

Figs. 45.16 and 45.17. World War II, Italy. HE on cotton cloth.

Fig. 45.18. World War II, Italy. HE on cotton miniature garrison cap patch.

Fig. 45.19. World War II, Italy. HE on satin.

Fig. 45.20. World War II, Italy. Bullion on wool.

Figs. 45.21 and 45.22. World War II, Italy. Bullion on wool with bullion border.

Fig. 45.23. World War II, Italy. Bullion on satin with bullion border applied to a twill base.

Fig. 45.24. World War II, Italy. Bullion on cotton patch with a bullion on wool "180 INF Thunder Bird 45 DIV" tab.

Fig. 45.25. World War II, England. FE, ODB.

Fig. 45.26. Post World War II, Germany. FE.

Fig. 45.27. Post World War II, Germany. Very unusual example with somewhat reversed colors. The patch is constructed of a sandwich of different satin materials. Just visible at the bottom right of the wing and tail are the guide lines hand drawn by the embroider.

Fig. 45.28. Post World War II, Germany. Cello cording on felt background embroidered to a wool base.

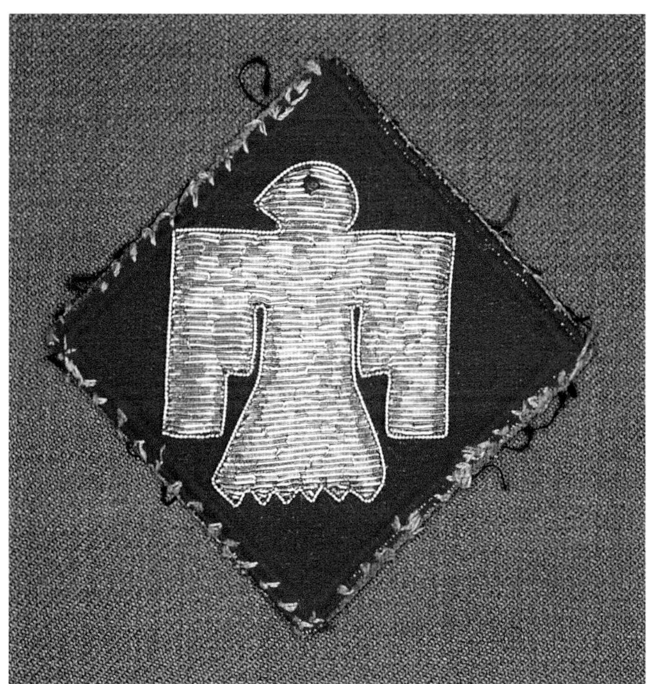

Fig. 45.29. Post World War II. U.S. made FE patch with German added bullion.

Fig. 45.30. Post World War II, Germany. Gold bullion cord on felt with bullion twist border.

Fig. 45.31. Post World War II. 1953 45th Division Christmas card.

Figs. 45.32 to 45.35. Post World War II, Japan. Four different all silk FE Japanese made patches.

Fig. 45.36. Post World War II, Japan. Bullion on felt.

Fig. 45.37. Post World War II, Japan. Bullion on felt with bullion border.

Fig. 45.38. Post World War II, Japan. Bullion on velvet right facing thunderbird.

Fig. 45.39. Post World War II, Japan. Bullion on silk quilted background.

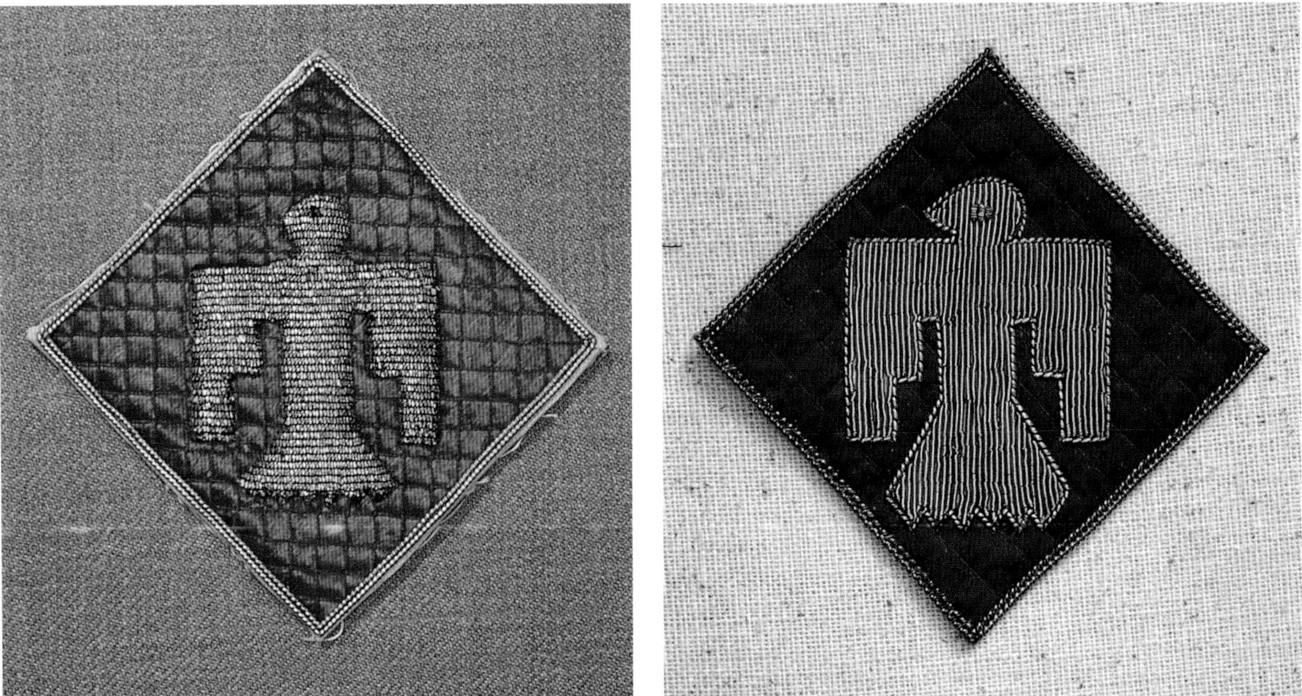

Figs. 45.40 and 45.41. Post World II, Japan. Bullion on quilted silk background with bullion border.

Fig. 45.42. Post World War II, Japan. Bullion on wool patch and nick name tab.

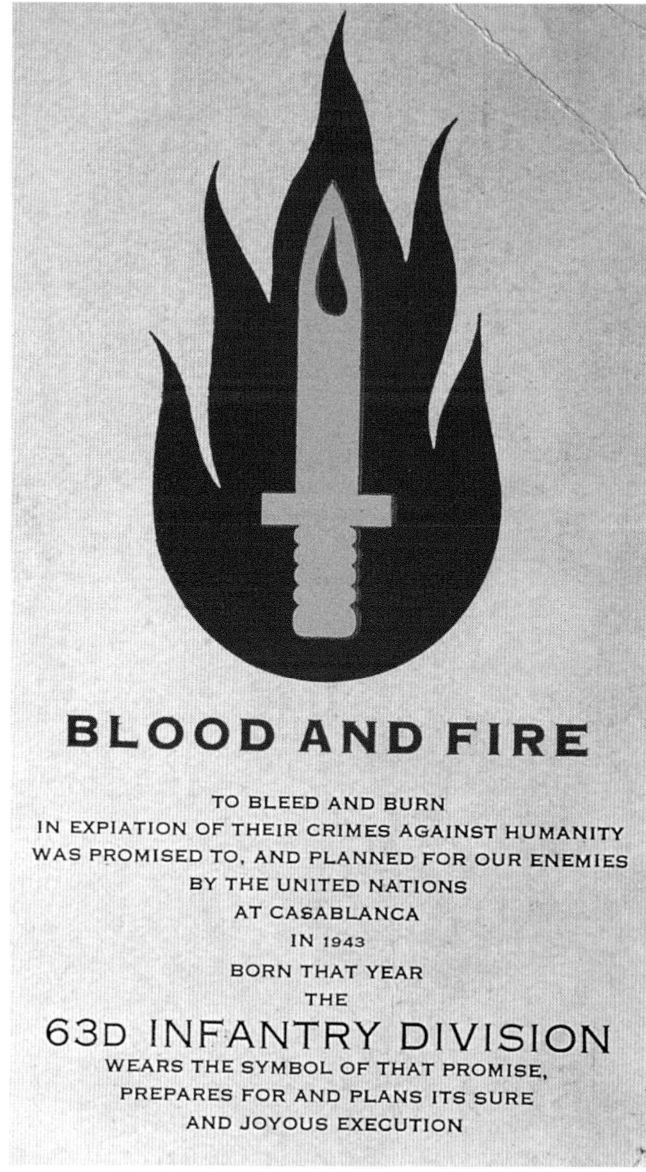

Fig. 63.1. World War II. 63rd Division postcard.

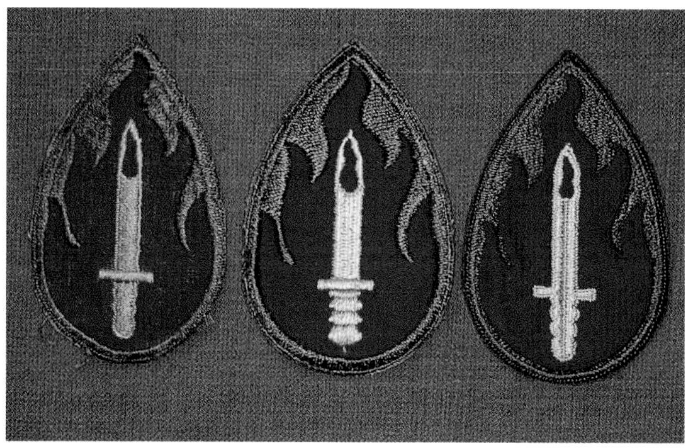

Fig. 63.2. World War II. Three different FE 63rd Division patches.

Fig. 63.3. World War II. FE white sword variation.

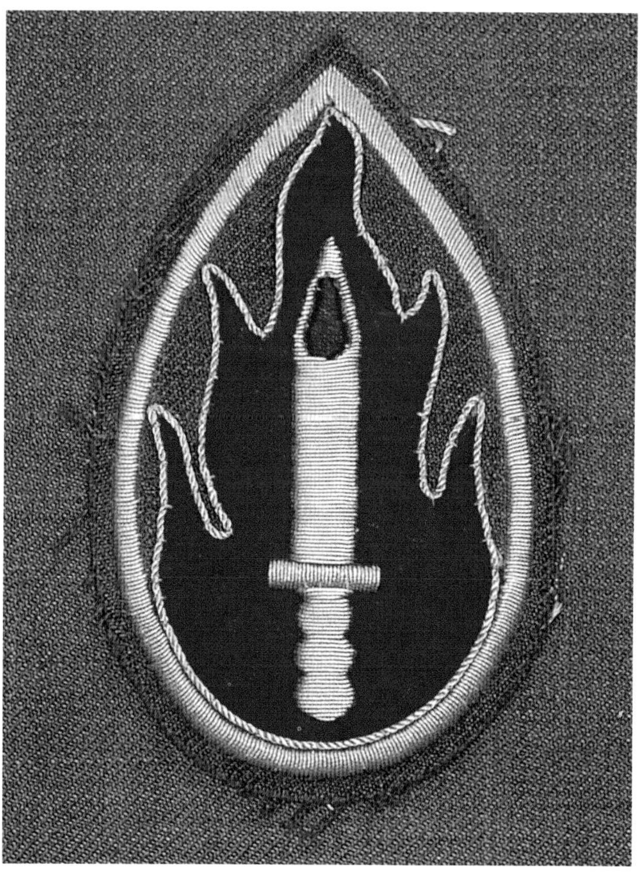

Fig. 63.4. Post World War II, Germany. Cello cording with felt flames applied to wool base.

Fig. 63.5. Post World War II, Germany. HE on wool with bullion cord border.

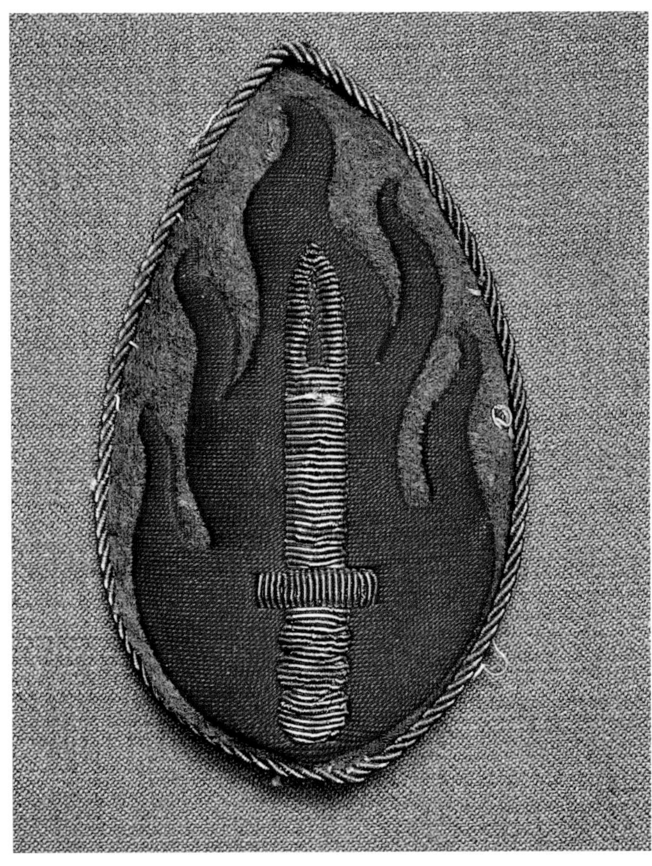

Fig. 63.6. Post World War II, Germany. HE on wool flames with bullion sword and border.

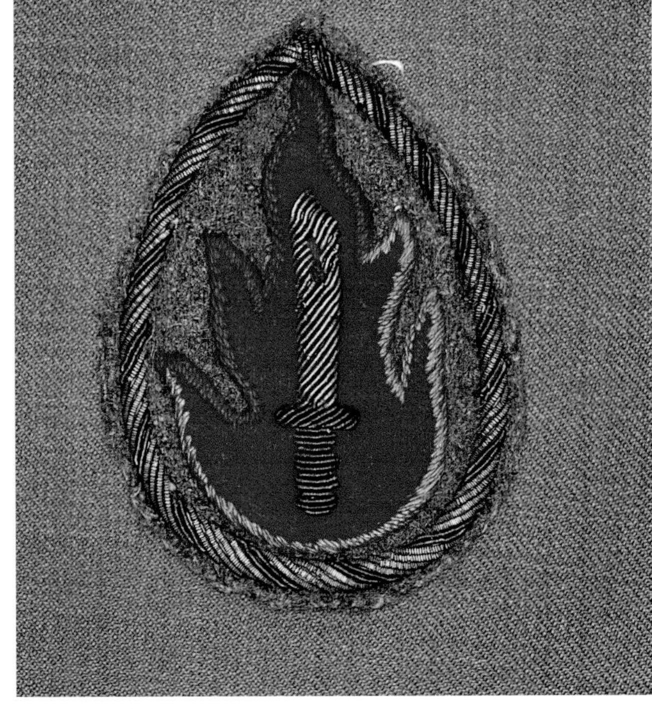

Fig. 63.7 and 63.8. Left and above: Post World War II, Germany. Felt flames applied to wool base with a bullion sword and border.

Fig. 63.9. Post World War II, Germany. Painted patch type DI, spring pin closure.

Fig. 63.10 and 63.11. Post World War II, Japan. FE.

Fig. 65.1. World War II. FE.

Fig. 65.2. Post World War II, Germany. FE.

Fig. 65.3. Post World War II, Germany. Felt on felt with bullion detail and border.

Fig. 65.4. Post World War II, Germany. Bullion cord on felt with HE border.

Fig. 65.5. Post World War II, Germany. Bullion cord on felt.

Figs. 66.1 and 66.2. World War II. FE. Two different first design 66th Division patches.

Fig. 66.3. World War II. FE. Second design or standard 66th Division. At the request of the division commander the patch was redesigned as he felt the running panther might be interpreted in a negative manner.

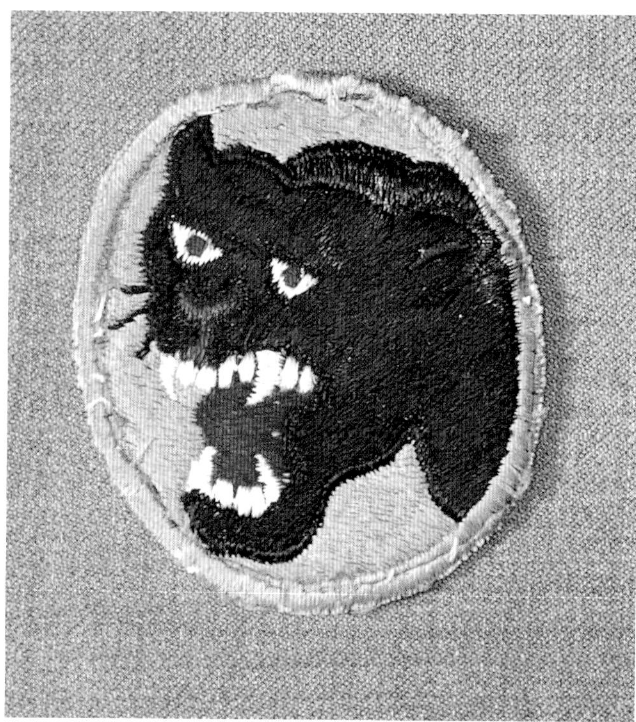

Fig. 66.4. World War II/Post World II, TM. Interesting variation with a yellow border. Fully embroidered all silk construction.

Fig. 66.5. Post World War II, Germany. FE white ear variation.

Fig. 66.6. Post World War II, Germany. HE on felt with bullion border.

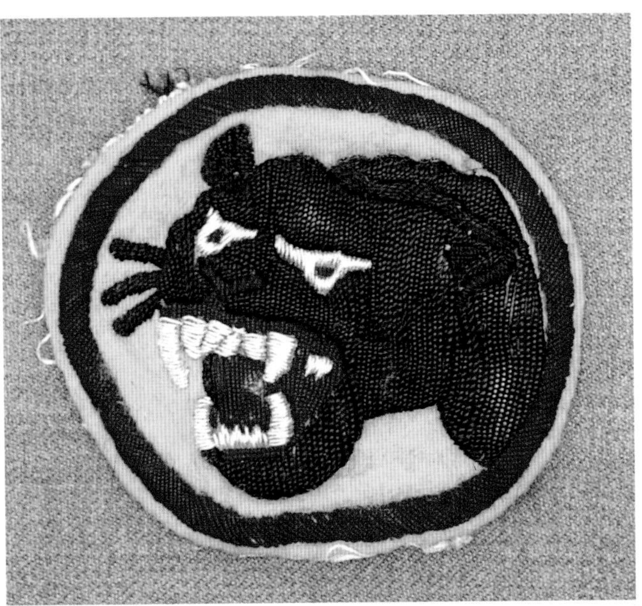

Fig. 66.7. Post World War II, Germany. HE on felt with bullion cord eyes and teeth.

Fig. 66.8. Post World War II, Germany. Felt panther applied to a tapestry like background with bullion cord border which is used to attach the other layers of material to a wool base.

Figs. 69.1 and 69.2. World War II. Three different examples of U.S. made 69th Division patches.

Fig. 69.3. World War II. FE. Here we have an unusual variation in which the design is missing the blue "9". Occasionally patches like this can be found with either errors in color or embroidered in all one color. These fall into two categories, one being manufacturers errors which would include color errors or reversals in the pattern (see ***Figs. 23.2, 29.14, 38.14.***). The second being "test shots" where manufactures would do a small run of patches to test the embroidery machine and to insure the design was being properly applied to the base material. The patches found in all one color are believed to fall into this category. Either variation makes an interesting addition to a collection.

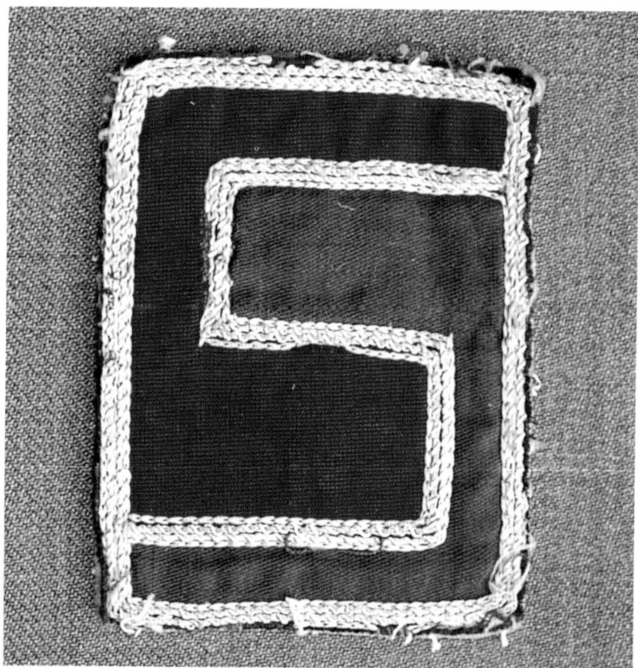

Fig. 69.4. World War II/Post World War II, Belgium. This patch is constructed of a sandwich of different layers of cotton material all sewn together with a fine chain stitch. The identification was made quite easy as this example still retains the makers label on the back.

Fig. 69.5. Post World War II, Germany. Satin and cotton embroidered together.

Fig. 69.6. Post world War II, Germany. HE on a twill base.

Fig. 69.7. Post World War II. Standard made U.S. patch with German added bullion.

Fig. 69.8. Post World War II, Germany. HE on felt with bullion border and detail.

Fig. 69.9. Post World War II, Germany. Miniature patch type painted DI. Spring pin closure.

Fig. 69.10. Post World War II, Germany. Small grouping of occupation made insignia. Painted patch type DI and Combat Infantry Badge and enameled 273rd Infantry Regiment DI's. All with spring pin closures.

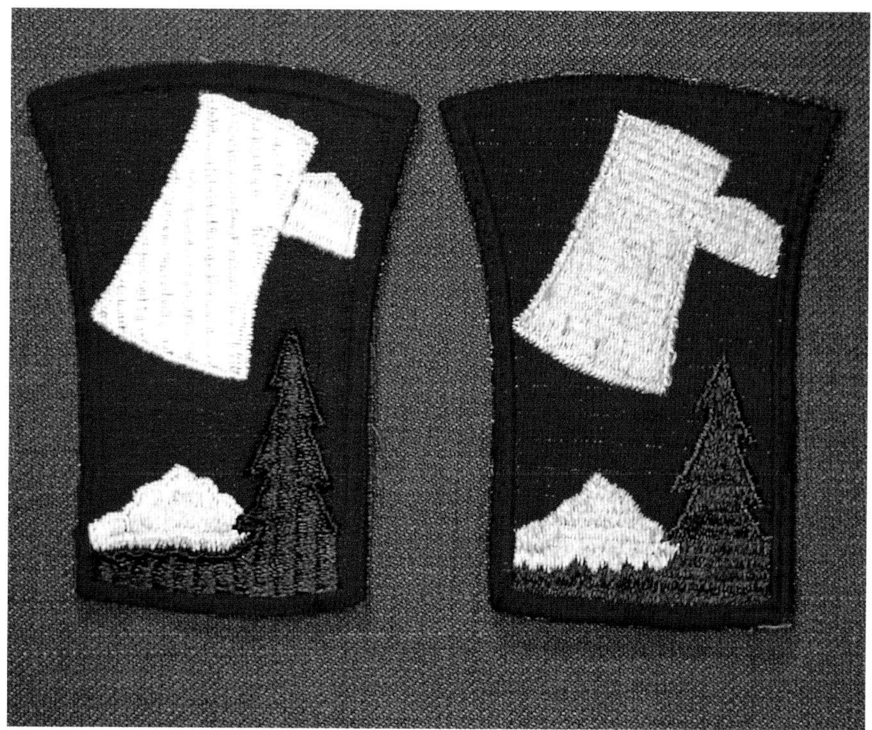

Fig. 70.1. World War II. FE.

Fig. 70.2. World War II. FE, ODB.

Fig. 70.3. World War II/Post World War II, TM. FE.

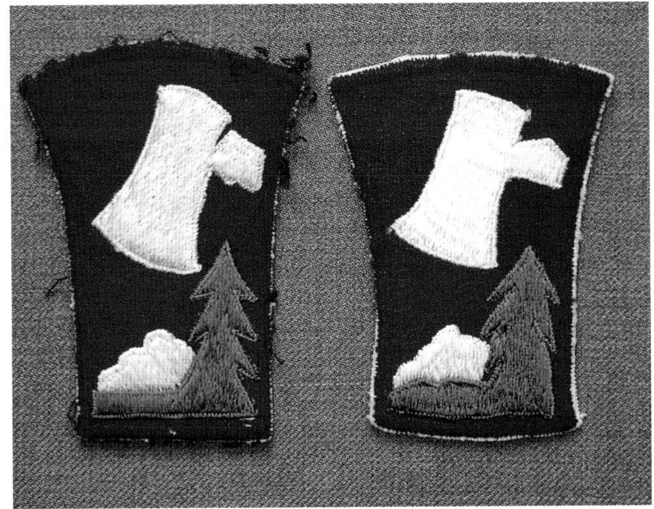

Fig. 70.4. Post World War II, Japan. Two different FE silk patches.

Fig. 70.5. Post World War II, Germany. HE on felt and wool with bullion detail.

Fig. 70.6. Post World War II, Germany. HE on wool with bullion detail and border.

Figs. 70.7 and 70.8. Post World War II, Germany. HE on felt with bullion detail and border.

Fig. 70.9. Post World War II, Germany. HE on velvet with bullion detail and border applied to a wool base.

Fig. 70.10. Post World War II, Germany. All bullion on cotton with HE border.

Fig. 71.1. World War II/Post World War II. Comparison of a U.S. made patch, left, and a German made patch, right.

Fig. 71.2. World War II. Twill.

Fig. 71.3. Post World War II, Germany. HE on felt and wool.

Figs. 71.4 and 71.5. Post World War II, Germany. HE on felt with bullion detail and cord twist border.

Fig. 71.6. Post World War II, Germany. HE on felt with bullion detail.

Fig. 71.7. Post World War II, Germany. HE on bullion cloth background and felt base.

Fig. 71.8. Post World War II, Germany. HE on aluminum tinsel cloth background and wool base.

Fig. 71.9. Post World War II, Germany. HE on felt with bullion cord background.

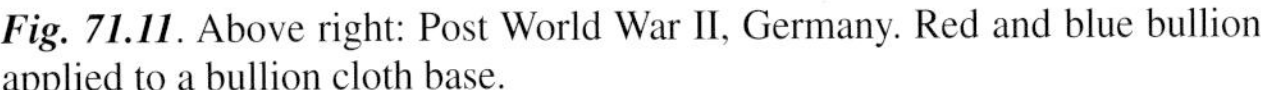

Fig. 71.10. Above: Post World War II, Germany. HE on bullion cloth background with red bullion border applied to a felt base.

Fig. 71.11. Above right: Post World War II, Germany. Red and blue bullion applied to a bullion cloth base.

Fig. 71.12. Right: Post World War II, Germany. 71st Division band. CS numerals with bullion detail with a ME border and lettering all on a bullion cloth background.

Fig. 75.1. World War II. Unidentified 75th Division Artilleryman.

Fig. 75.2. World War II. FE. Note how the first example has outlined letters and the second does not.

Fig. 75.3. Post World War II, Germany. FE.

Fig. 75.4. Post World War II, Germany. HE on felt background with a bullion border applied to a twill base.

Fig. 75.5. Post World War II, Germany. HE on felt with bullion detail.

Fig. 75.6. Post World War II, Germany. HE on felt with bullion center stripe and detail and a double cello cord border all on a felt base.

Fig. 75.7. Post World War II, Germany. HE on felt with a bullion center stripe and detail with a bullion border all on a felt base.

Fig. 76.1. World War I. Wool on wool construction.

Fig. 76.2. World War I. Wool on wool with ribbon tape and HE detail.

Fig. 76.3. World War I. Wool on wool with bullion detail.

Fig. 76.4. World War I. ME on felt. Alternate 76th Division "Liberty Bell" design.

Fig. 76.5. World War I. HE on wool.

Fig. 76.6. World War I. Yet another design employed by the 76th Division during World War I was a sailing ship superimposed on a star. Wool on wool with HE detail.

Fig. 76.7. Interwar. ME on wool.

Fig. 76.8. World War II/Post World War II. FE. Comparison of three different 76th Division patches. First example features a green cross bar. The second, a silver cross bar and the third features a white cross bar. The white bar example is most likely a post World War II variant.

Fig. 76.9. World War II/Post World War II, TM. FE. Front and back of an interesting variation with a grey-green border. The red and blue fields have a woven texture and the remaining design elements are embroidered.

Fig. 76.10. Post World War II, Germany. HE on felt.

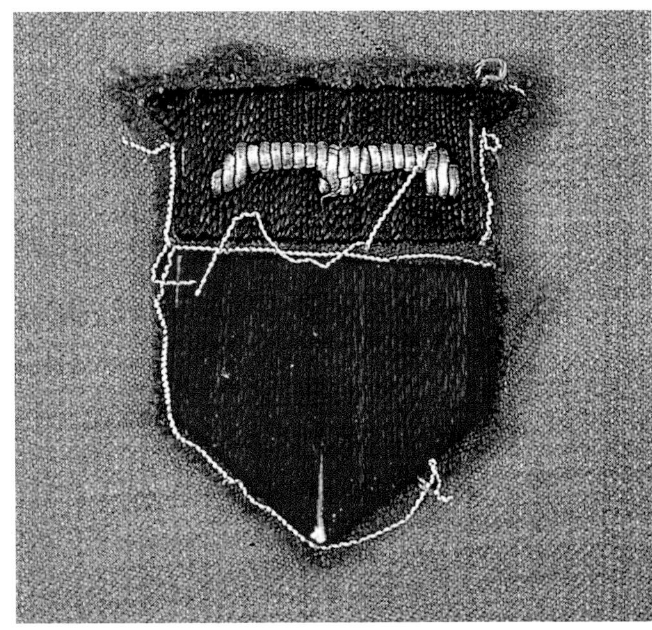

Fig. 76.11. Post World War II, Germany. HE on wool with bullion detail.

Fig. 76.12. Post World War II, Germany. Felt embroidered to a wool base with bullion detail.

Fig. 76.13. Post World War II, Germany. Bullion on felt with a bullion twist border.

Fig. 77.1. World War I. Unidentified 77th Division doughboy wearing a felt on felt patch. The design features the Statue of Liberty flanked by 7 and 7 representing the unit's numerical designation.

Fig. 77.2. World War I. Felt on felt patch of the same design being worn in *Fig. 77.1*.

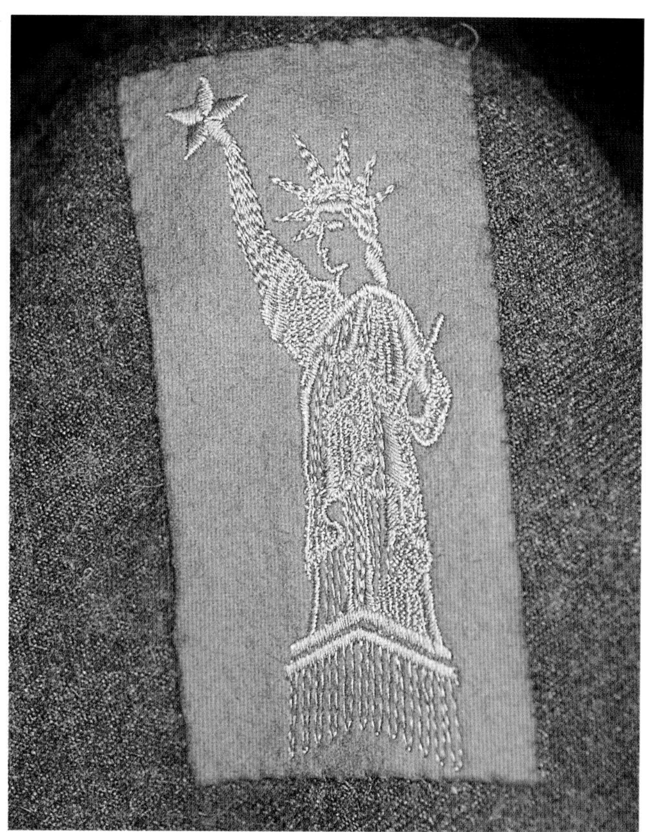

Fig. 77.3. World War I. Corporal Carl W. Hanson, 302nd Engineer Regt., Co. A. ME on felt. This design features a star in Lady Liberty's hand in lieu of the torch.

Fig. 77.4. World War I. ME on silk.

Fig. 77.5. World War I. ME on a woven background.

Fig. 77.6. World War I. HE on a woven background.

Fig. 77.7. World War I. CS and cotton cording applied to a wool base.

Fig. 77.8. World War I. Seven doughboys from the 308th Infantry Regiment.

Fig. 77.9. World War I. ME on wool. This patch features a 3/4 view of the Statue of Liberty.

Fig. 77.11. World War I. HE on wool.

Fig. 77.10. World War I. ME on wool. This picture gives the reader some clue as to how the patches were manufactured and distributed to the soldiers. Fortunately the doughboy didn't take the time to sew these patches to his jacket and overcoat.

Fig. 77.12. World War I. Liberty Loan star in hand variation.

Fig. 77.13. World War I. Liberty Loan.

Fig. 77.14. World War I. Liberty Loan. Star in hand variation with "77th N.Y. Division U.S.A." below.

Fig. 77.15. World War I. Liberty Loan with "77th Division" below. This patch and ***Fig. 77.14*** may have been originally intended as welcome home ribbons but have been modified for use as shoulder patches. See ***Figs. 27.7*** and ***42.18*** for examples of welcome home ribbons.

Fig. 77.16. World War I. An unidentified Dentist from the 77th Division wearing a bullion patch.

Figs. 77.17 to 77.20. World War I. Bullion on silk.

Fig. 77.21. World War I. Bullion on wool with bullion border.

Fig. 77.22. World War I. Bullion on cotton cloth.

Fig. 77.23. World War I. Unidentified 77th Division doughboy with the division insignia painted on his helmet. This obviously is a reversed image as no M-1917 Enfield rifle had a left hand bolt!

Fig. 77.24. World War I. Stencil on wool. It is unsure if this was intended as a shoulder patch.

Fig. 77.25. World War I/Interwar. ME on felt.

Fig. 77.26. World War I/Interwar. ME on felt applied to a wool base. Star in hand variation.

Figs. 77.27 and 77.28. Interwar. Woven.

Fig. 77.29. World War II. Four different examples of U.S. made FE patches.

Fig. 77.30. World War II. FE. Light blue background variation.

Figs. 77.31 and 77.32. World War II. FE, ODB.

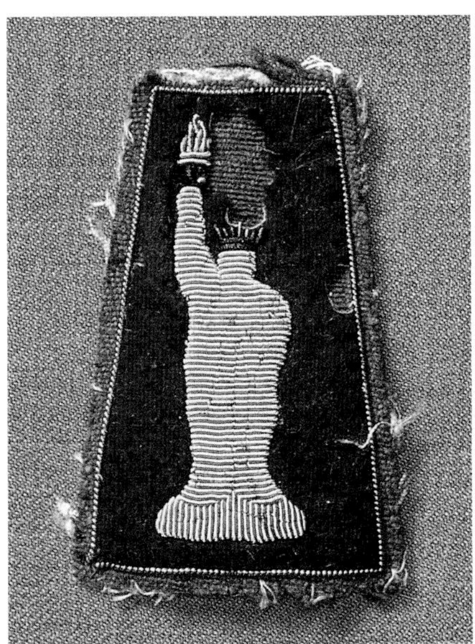

Fig. 77.33. Post World War II, Japan. Bullion on felt applied to a wool base.

Fig. 78.1. World War I. Pvt. Carl E. Griffin, 311th Infantry, Co. B, wearing a no lightning bolt 78th Division patch.

Fig. 78.2. World War I. Pvt. Griffin's no bolt 78th Division patch pasted in his war time scrapbook.

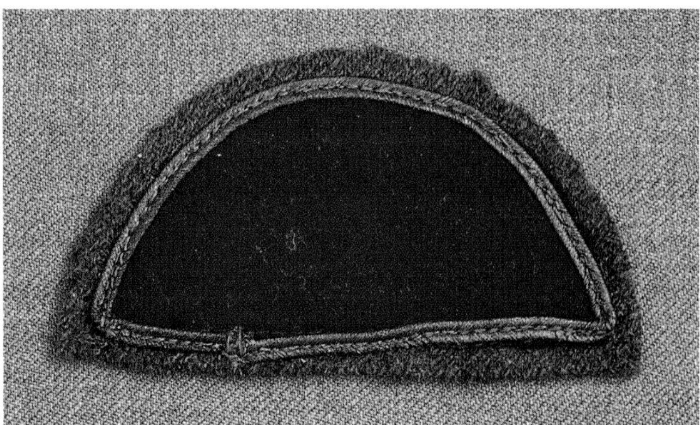

Fig. 78.3. World War I. Felt on wool with bullion soutache border.

Fig. 78.4. World War I. A very nicely rendered pencil sketch of Pvt. Griffin.

Fig. 78.6. World War I. Corporal Charles B. Clough, 303rd Ammo Train, Co.C.

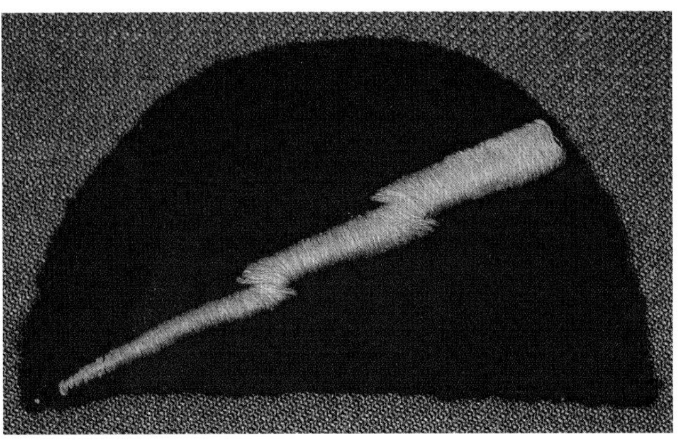

Fig. 78.5. Left: World War I. Another of Pvt. Griffin's patches. HE on wool.

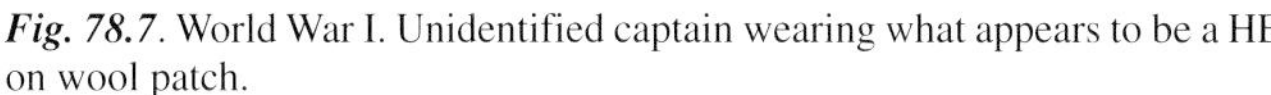

Fig. 78.7. World War I. Unidentified captain wearing what appears to be a HE on wool patch.

Figs. 78.8 to 78.10. Left and two below: World War I. HE on wool.

Fig. 78.11. World War I. Another photo of Corporal Clough.

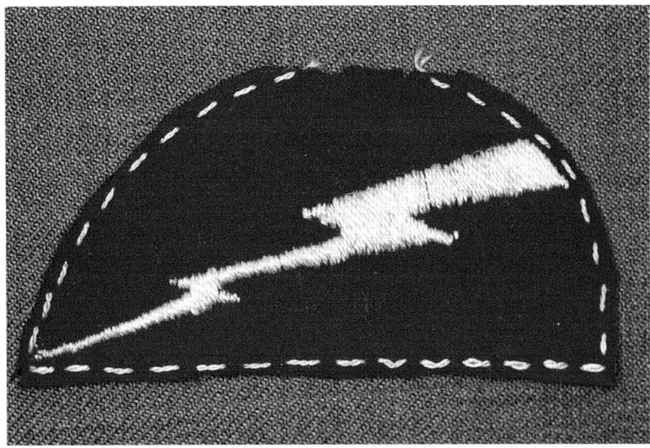

Fig. 78.12. World War I. Corporal Clough's HE on wool patch. The embroidered dashed outline was used as a guide when cutting a single patch from a larger sheet of patches.

Figs. 78.13 to 78.15. Above and two below: World War I. Bullion on wool.

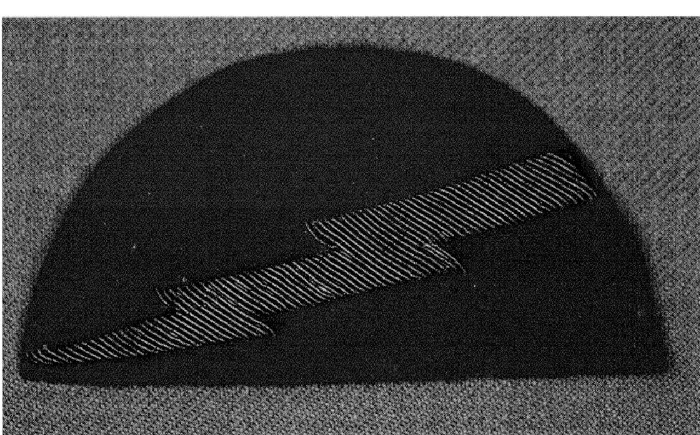

Fig. 78.16. World War I. Unidentified 78th Division Artilleryman wearing a variant 78th Division patch featuring a white border and multiple ascending lightning bolts.

Fig. 78.17. World War I. Two unidentified doughboys each wearing another white border variation, this time featuring descending lightning bolts.

Fig. 78.18. World War I. HE on wool with descending lightning bolts. This exact design has been observed in ascending form as well.

Fig. 78.19. World War I. Another unusual descending lightning bolt variation, comprised of multiple layers of wool.

Fig. 78.21. Interwar. HE on felt.

Fig. 78.20. Left: World War I. Liberty Loan.

Fig. 78.22. Interwar. Similar patch to ***Fig. 78.21***, but being worn backwards!

Fig. 78.23. World War I?/Interwar. ME on felt.

Fig. 78.24. World War II. FE.

Figs. 78.25 and 78.26. Above and below: World War II. FE. Two different red border variations.

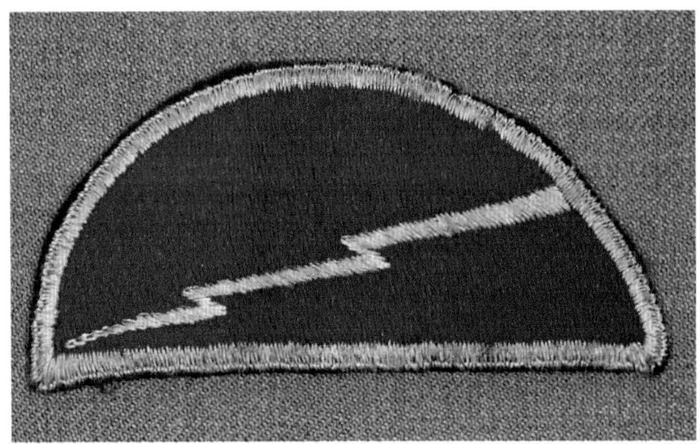

Fig. 78.27. World War II, England. FE.

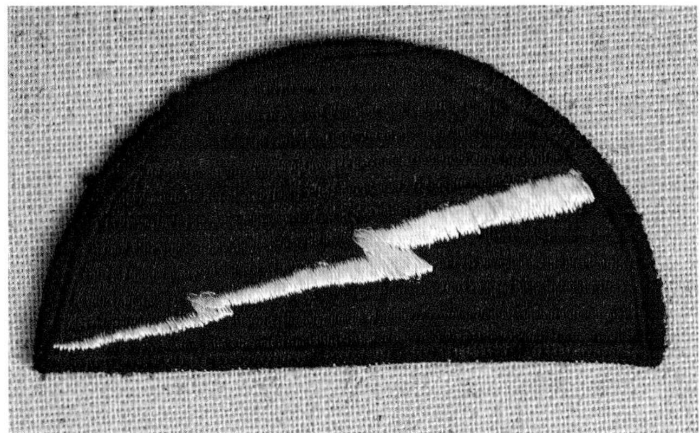

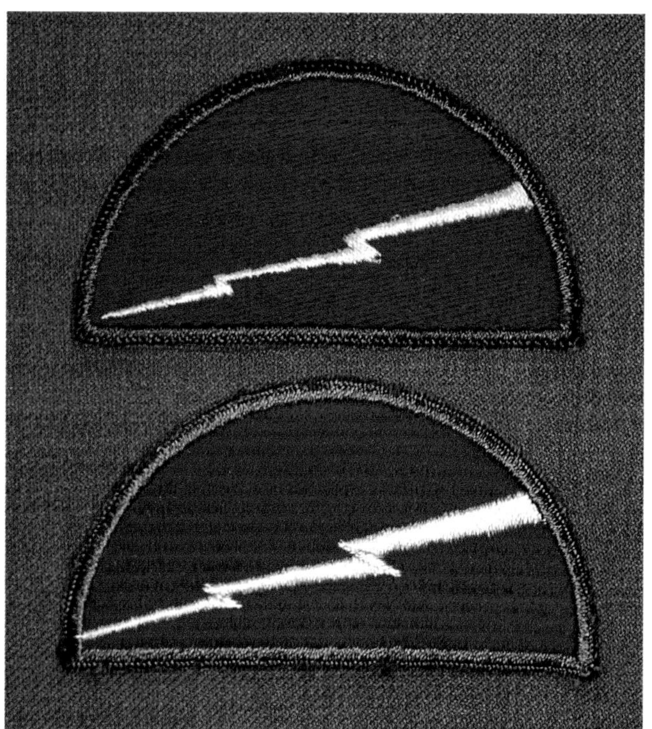

Fig. 78.28. World War II/Post World War II. Comparison of two FE patches. German made top, U.S. made bottom.

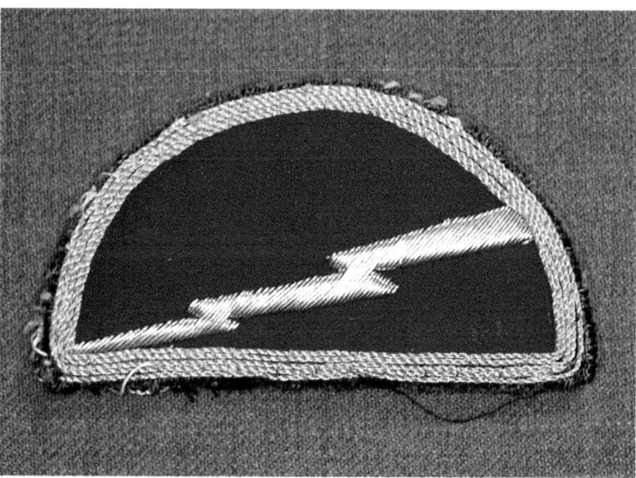

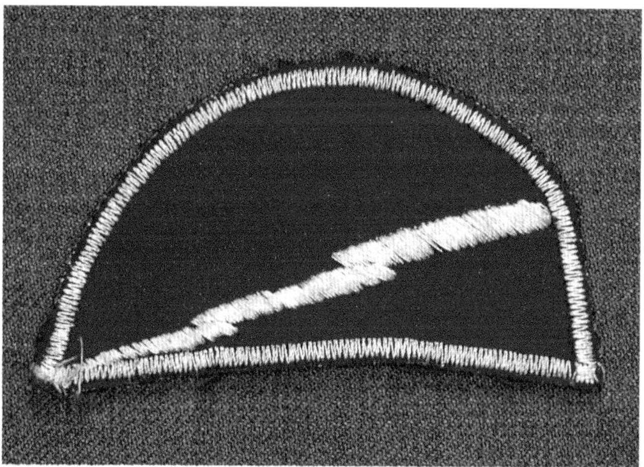

Fig. 78.29. Post World War II, Germany. ME on cotton.

Figs. 78.30 and 78.31. Above and below: Post World War II, Germany. Front and back of an interesting German made variation complete with manufacturer's stamp. ME on satin finish cotton cloth.

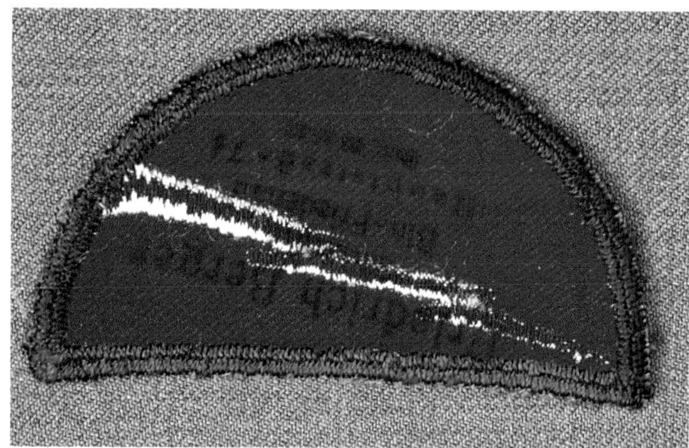

Figs. 78.32. and 78.33. Two at left: Post World War II. German added bullion and cello cording over a U.S. made patch.

Fig. 78.34. Post World War II, Germany. Bullion lightning bolt and corded border on cotton.

Fig. 78.35. Post World War II, German. HE on felt with bullion border

Figs. 78.36 and 78.37. Post World War II, Germany. Bullion on cotton.

Figs. 78.38 and 78.39. Post World War II, Germany. Bullion on wool.

Fig. 78.40. Post World War II, Japan. Fully hand embroidered in silk.

Fig. 78.41. Post World War II, Germany. HE on wool with added "311th", designating one of the division's three infantry regiments.

Fig. 78.42. Post World War II, Germany. Bullion and cello cording on felt with integral "Lightning" nickname tab.

Fig. 78.43. Post World War II, Germany. FE 78th Division patch with integral "Lightning" and "309th Inf" tabs.

Fig. 78.44. Right: Post World War II, Germany. Bullion on wool 78th Division patch with integral "Lightning" and "309 Inf" tabs.

Fig. 79.1. World War I. Unidentified 79th Division doughboy with a Cross of Lorraine pin on his garrison cap.

Fig. 79.2. World War I. Unidentified 79th Division doughboy from Machine Gun Co. A, wearing an applied felt or wool patch.

Fig. 79.3. World War I. Wool on wool.

Fig. 79.4. World War I. Felt on felt.

Fig. 79.5. Left: World War I. Wool on wool with a soutache border.

Fig. 79.6. World War I. Unidentified 79th Division, 316th Infantry Regiment doughboy wearing an embroidered patch.

Fig. 79.7. World War I. HE on wool.

Figs. 79.08 to 79.10. Below and two at right: World War I. ME on felt.

Fig. 79.11. World War I. Another nice image of a doughboy wearing an embroidered style patch.

Fig. 79.12. World War I. ME on wool.

Fig. 79.14. World War I. Interesting image of two doughboys, one wearing his 79th Division patch on his shirt pocket.

Fig. 79.13. Left: World War I. Liberty Loan.

Fig. 79.15. World War I. Bullion CS on wool.

Fig. 79.16. World War I. Bullion cord HE on wool.

Figs. 79.17 and 79.18. World War I. Bullion on wool.

Fig. 79.19. Interwar. HE on wool.

Figs. 79.20 and 79.21. Interwar. ME on wool.

Figs. 79.22 and 79.23. Interwar. ME on navy blue felt.

Fig. 79.24. World War II. FE.

Fig. 79.25. World War II/Post World War II, TM? FE. Somewhat unusual patch with a woven-like background.

Figs. 79.26 to 79.29. World War II/Post World War II, France? FE. Crudely machine embroidered with some silk components, these patches are believed to show the characteristics of French embroidery patterns including a thin raised border.

Fig. 79.30. World War II/Post World War II, TM. FE.

Fig. 79.31. Post World War II, Germany. FE.

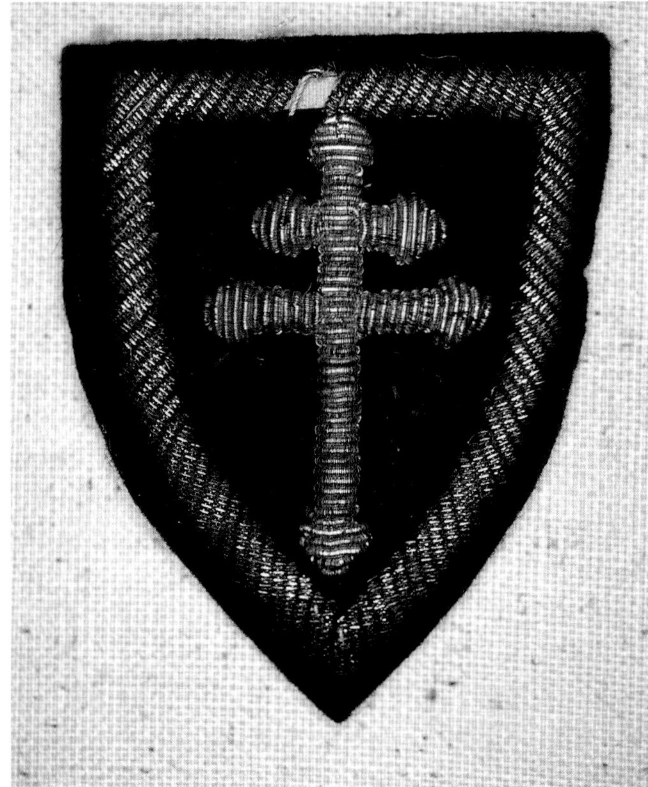

Figs. 79.32 and 79.33. Post World War II, Germany. Bullion on felt.

Fig. 79.34. Post World War II, Germany. Bullion on satin with a HE border.

Fig. 79.35. Post World War II, Japan. Bullion on quilted silk background.

Fig. 79.36. World War I. Hand carved box featuring the 79th Division insignia.

Fig. 79.37. Interwar. 1926 reunion badge for the 79th Division. The center area in the metal frame would hold the name of the reunion attendee.

Fig. 80.1. World War I. Unidentified doughboy from the HQ Co. of the 313th Field Artillery regiment wearing an embroidered style patch.

Figs. 80.2 to 80.4. Above and below left: World War I. HE on wool.

Fig. 80.5. World War I. Unidentified doughboy of the 320th Infantry Regiment wearing a patch similar to ***Figs. 80.2*** through ***80.4***.

Figs. 80.6 and 80.7. World War I. ME on felt

Fig. 80.8. World War I. Another 80th Division doughboy wearing a patch similar to ***Figs 80.6 and 80.7***.

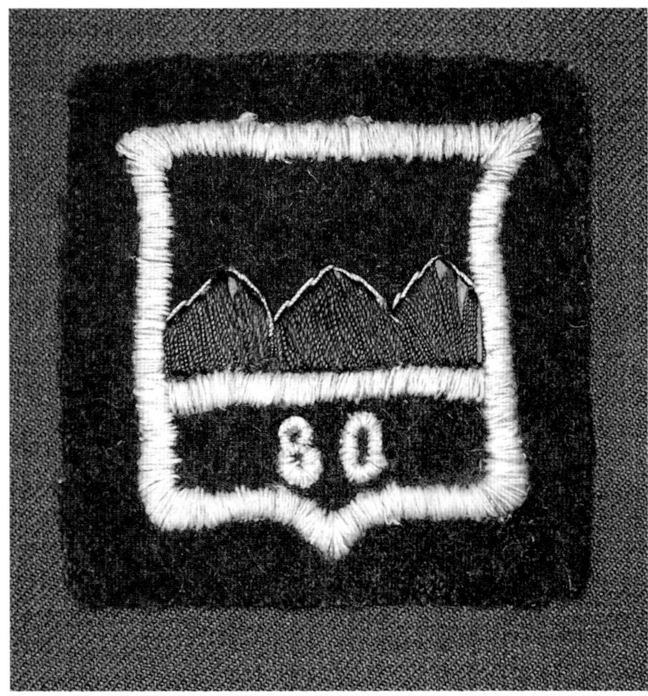

Fig. 80.9. World War I. HE on wool with the unit numerical designation sewn beneath the mountains.

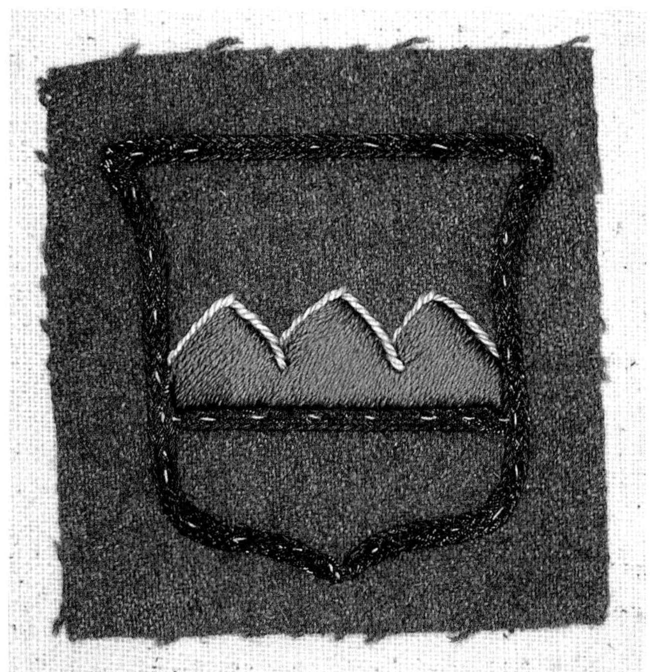

Figs. 80.10 and 80.11. World War I. HE on wool with bullion soutache border.

Fig. 80.12. World War I. Miniature garrison cap patch. HE on wool with bullion soutache border.

Fig. 80.13. World War I. Dan Barton's velvet on wool with bullion soutache border patch.

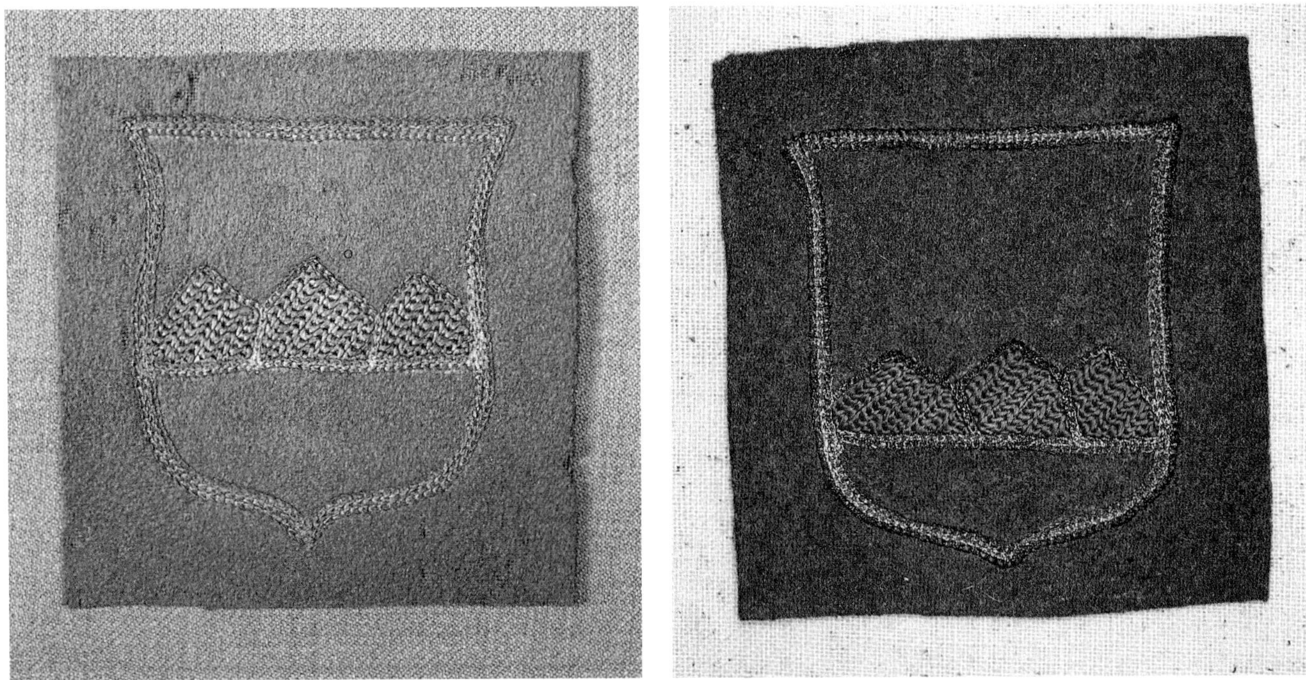

Figs. 80.14 and 80.15. World War I. CS and bullion CS on wool.

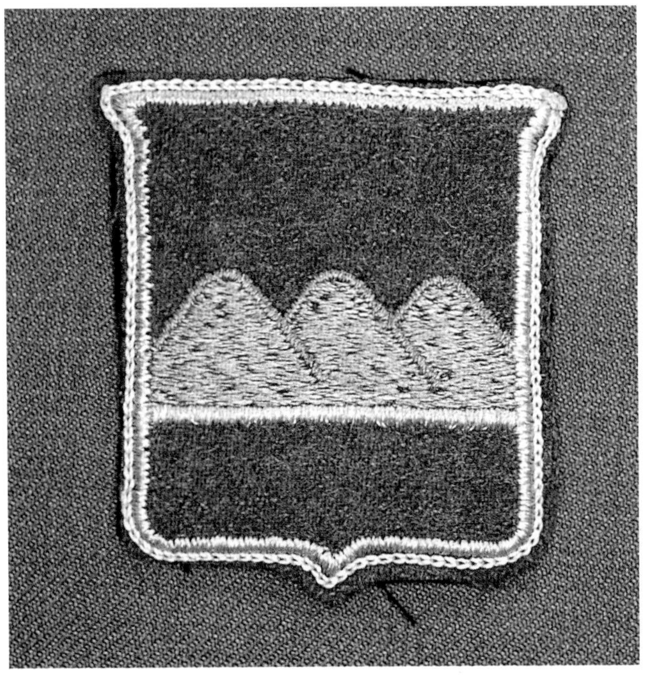

Fig. 80.16. Interwar. ME on wool with a CS border used to attach a felt backing.

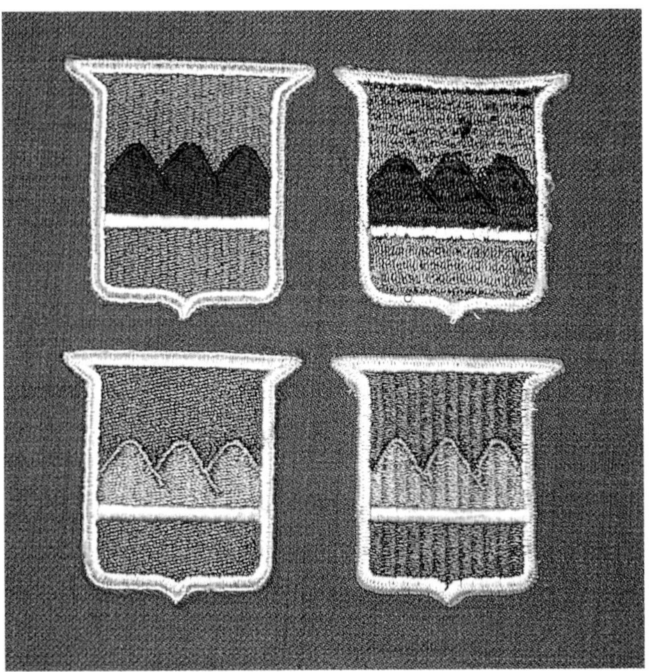

Fig. 80.17. World War II. Four different FE patches.

Fig. 80.18. Post World War II, Germany. FE.

Fig. 80.19. Post World War II, Germany. ME on officer's dark OD wool elastique.

Fig. 80.20. Post World War II, Germany. HE on felt.

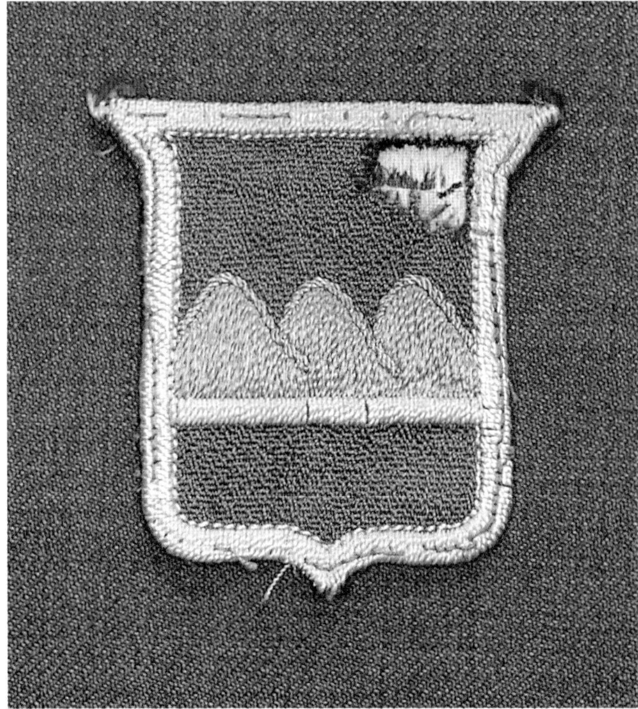

Fig. 80.21. Post World War II, Germany. HE on satin.

Fig. 80.22. Post World War II, Germany. HE on officer's dark OD wool elastique.

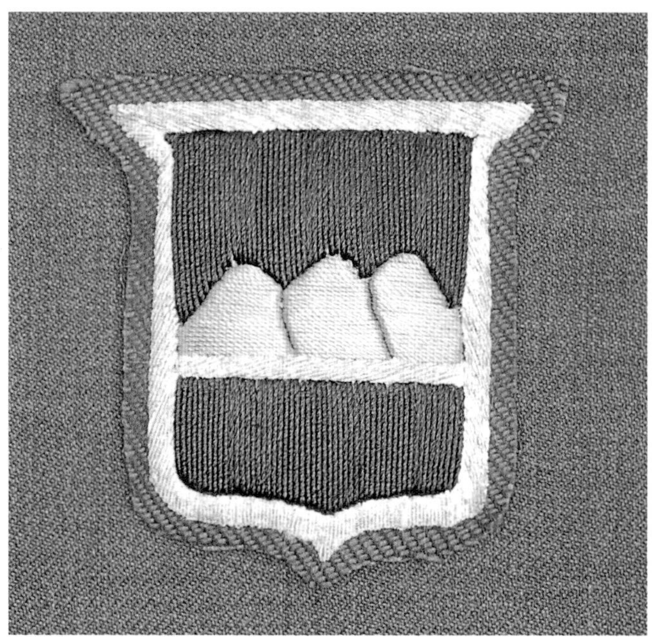

Fig. 80.23. Post World War II, Germany. HE on twill with bullion crossbar and border.

Fig. 80.24. Post World War II, Germany. HE on wool with bullion crossbar and border.

Fig. 80.25. Post World War II, Germany. Bullion tapestry background with bullion detail and border all on a wool base.

Fig. 80.26. Post World War II, Korea. ME on satin and cotton.

Fig. 80.27. Post World War II, Germany. Enameled patch type DI with spring pin closure, made by Poellath.

Fig. 81.1. World War I. Unidentified 81st Division doughboy of either the 161st or 162nd Infantry Brigade. Like other divisions during World War I, the 81st employed a color coded system to identify different units within the division. However some colors were used by more than one unit and on occasion errors in use can be found. One example observed was an identified Infantry uniform that had a red Wildcat. The two color schemes that are not illustrated used by the division are: Buff – 306th Supply Train, and Green – 306th Sanitary Train.

Fig. 81.2. World War I. ME on felt. Black was used for the division HQ, MG battalions and the 306th Engineer Regiment.

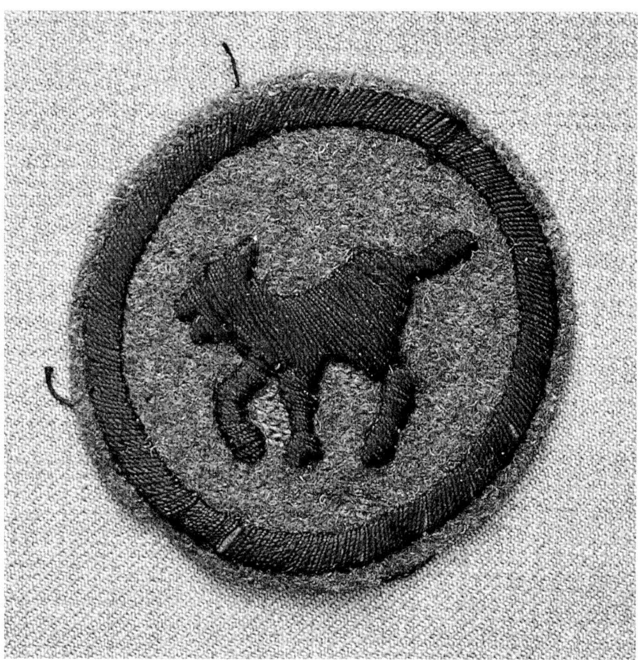

Fig. 81.3. World War I. ME on wool. HQ, MG battalions and the 306th Eng.

Fig. 81.4. World War I. 161st Infantry Brigade. Felt on felt.

Figs. 81.5 and 81.6. World War I. 162nd Infantry Brigade. Wool on wool.

Fig. 81.7. World War I. A faded 162nd Infantry Brigade. Felt on felt.

Fig. 81.8. World War I. 162nd Infantry Brigade. ME on felt.

Fig. 81.9. World War I. 162nd Infantry Brigade. Liberty Loan.

Figs. 81.10 and 81.11. Above and below: World War I. 156th Field Artillery Brigade or Ammunition Train. Felt on felt.

Fig. 81.12. World War I. 156th Field Artillery Brigade or Ammunition Train. Wool on wool.

Figs. 81.13 and 81.14. World War I. 156th Field Artillery Brigade or Ammunition Train. ME on felt. ***Fig. 81.14*** is most likely just a color variation or manufacture's error and not a different unit.

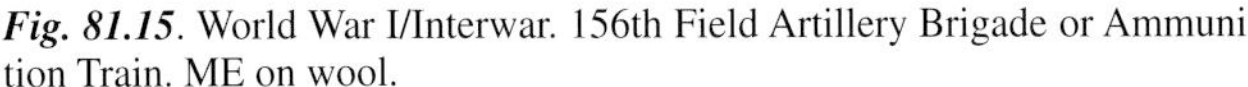

Fig. 81.15. World War I/Interwar. 156th Field Artillery Brigade or Ammunition Train. ME on wool.

Fig. 81.16. World War I. 306th Signal Battalion. Liberty Loan.

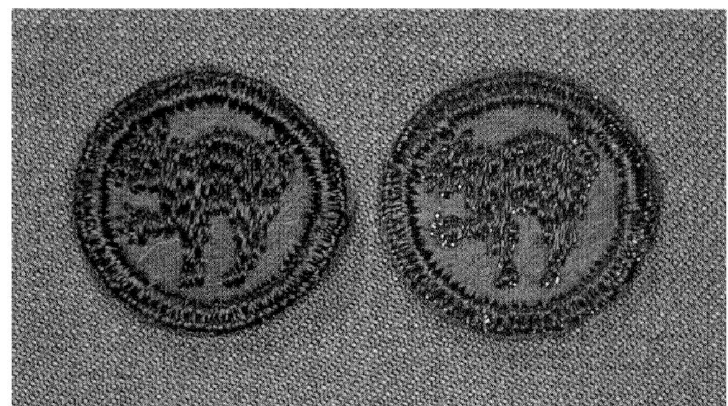

Fig. 81.17. World War I. Miniature garrison cap patches for the 162nd Inf. Bde., left, and the 156th FA Bde. or Ammo Train, right. ME on felt.

Fig. 81.19. World War II/Post World War II. Four different FE 81st Division patches. The particular style of OD border shown at bottom right is believed to be Post World War II, as it has been observed on several Post World War II fatigue shirts.

Fig. 81.20. World War II. FE, ODB.

Fig. 81.18. World War II. Unidentified GI wearing a FE 81st Division shoulder patch.

Fig. 81.21. World War II. FE with hand added red tongue.

Fig. 81.22. Post World War II, Japan. FE.

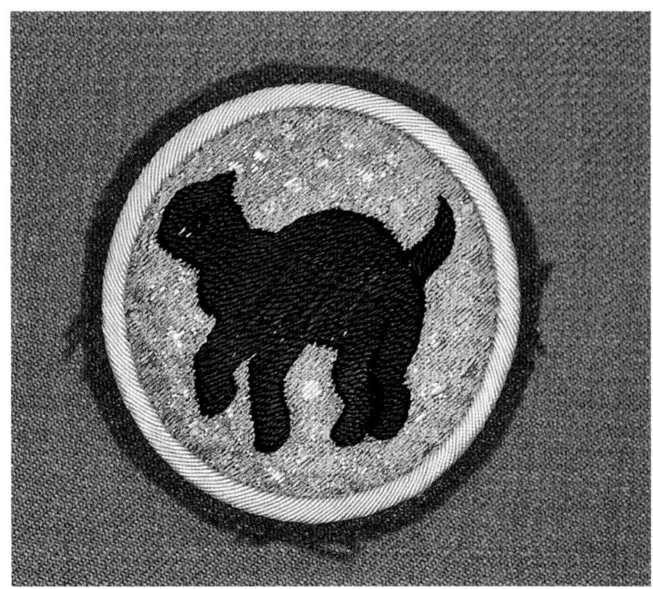

Fig. 81.23. Post World War II, Germany. HE on tapestry background with cello border on a wool base.

Fig. 81.24. Post World War II, Germany. HE on red wool with a bullion border applied to a wool base with a ME border.

Fig. 81.25. Post World War II, Germany. HE on felt with a bullion border.

Fig. 82.1. World War I. Unidentified 82nd Division doughboy wearing a soutache on wool patch.

Figs. 82.2 and 82.3. Two above: World War I. HE on wool.

Figs. 82.4 to 82.6. Above and two at right: World War I. ME on felt. Patches with yellow or gold elements are usually considered officer's patches. However in reality they were used by both officers and enlisted personnel.

Fig. 82.7. World War I. Unidentified Infantry Pvt. wearing a patch similar to ***Fig. 82.6***.

Figs. 82.8 and 82.9. Above and below: World War I. Liberty Loan.

Fig. 82.10. World War I. White soutache on wool.

Fig. 82.11. World War I. Pvt. Morton Crevoiserat, Co. A, 325th Infantry Regiment. Red, white and blue soutache on wool.

Fig. 82.12. World War I. Gold soutache on wool.

Fig. 82.13. World War I. Red, white and blue soutache on velvet.

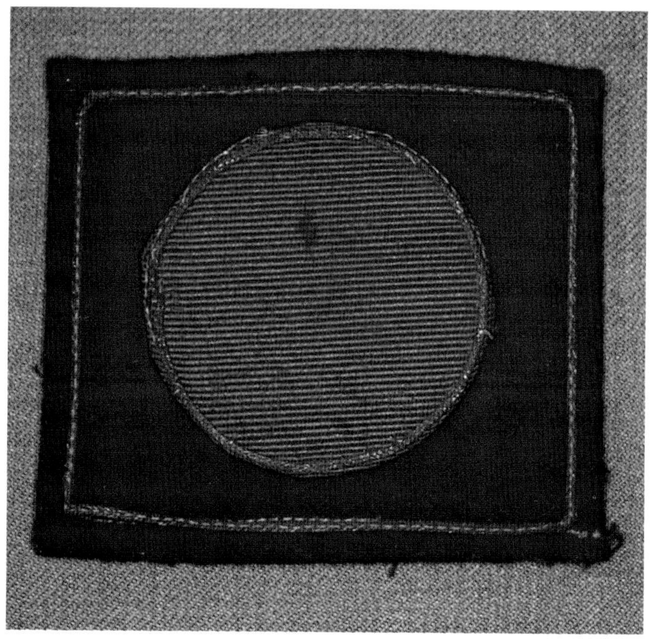

Fig. 82.14. World War I. Blue ribbon field on wool with bullion borders. Occasionally World War I 82nd Division patches can be found without the "AA" (All American) monogram.

Figs. 82.15 to 82.17. Above and two below: World War I. Bullion soutache on wool.

Figs. 82.18 and 82.19. World War I. Bullion soutache on wool.

Figs. 82.20 and 82.21. World War I. Bullion soutache on velvet.

Fig. 82.22. World War I. Bullion cord on woven field applied to a wool base with bullion borders.

Fig. 82.23. World War I. Bullion on wool.

Fig. 82.24. World War II. A group of unidentified Paratroopers relaxing in a café.

Fig. 82.25. World War II. FE.

Figs. 82.26 and 82.27. World War II. FE with integral Airborne tab.

Fig. 82.28. World War II, England. Front and back comparison of an English made FE patch.

Fig. 82.29. World War II, TM? ME on felt with a separately added U.S. made FE tab.

Fig. 82.30. World War II, England. ME on felt Airborne tab.

Fig. 82.31. Post World War II. Private R. Bicknell, Division Headquarters. The colors of the parachute oval are from the outside in: blue, white and red.

Fig. 82.32. Post World War II, Japan. FE.

Fig. 82.33. Post World War II. U.S. made FE patch with German added bullion.

Fig. 82.34. Post World War II, Germany. ME on velvet with ME bullion.

Fig. 82.35. Post World War II, Germany. Bullion on felt.

Fig. 82.36. Post World War II, Japan. Bullion on felt applied to a twill base.

Fig. 82.37. World War I. HE on wool collar disk patch. This insignia was probably intended to be worn on the garrison cap or collar. The color scheme and design mirror that of the divisional patch.

Fig. 83.1. World War I. Unidentified doughboy from the 331st Infantry Regiment wearing a bullion on wool patch.

Fig. 83.2. World War I. CS on felt.

Figs. 83.3 and 83.4. Above and below: World War I. Bullion on wool.

Fig. 83.5. World War I. Bullion soutache on wool

Fig. 83.6. World War I/Interwar. ME on wool

Fig. 83.7. World War II. FE, ODB.

Fig. 83.8. World War I. FE. White monogram variation.

Fig. 83.9. Post World War II, Germany. FE.

Fig. 83.10. Far left: Post World War II, Germany. HE cello cording on felt and wool.

Fig. 83.11. Left: Post World War II, Germany. Cello monogram on felt with black bullion border.

Fig. 83.12. Post World War II, Germany. FE "Thunderbolt" nickname tab.

Fig. 83.13. Post World War II, Germany. HE on silk "Thunderbolt" nickname tab.

Fig. 83.14. Post World War II, Germany. HE on felt nickname tab over a U.S. made FE patch.

Fig. 84.1. World War I. Unidentified 84th Division doughboy.

Fig. 84.2. World War I. Simplest of the 84th Division patch designs, a wool cut out of an axe.

Fig. 84.3. World War I. FE on felt.

Fig. 84.4. World War I. ME on wool with unit nickname and numerical designation. During World War I the division was known as the "Lincoln" Division after President Abraham Lincoln who counted splitting rails among his many professions.

Fig. 84.5. World War I. Bullion on wool.

Fig. 84.6. World War I. Bullion on wool with a HE border applied to a wool base.

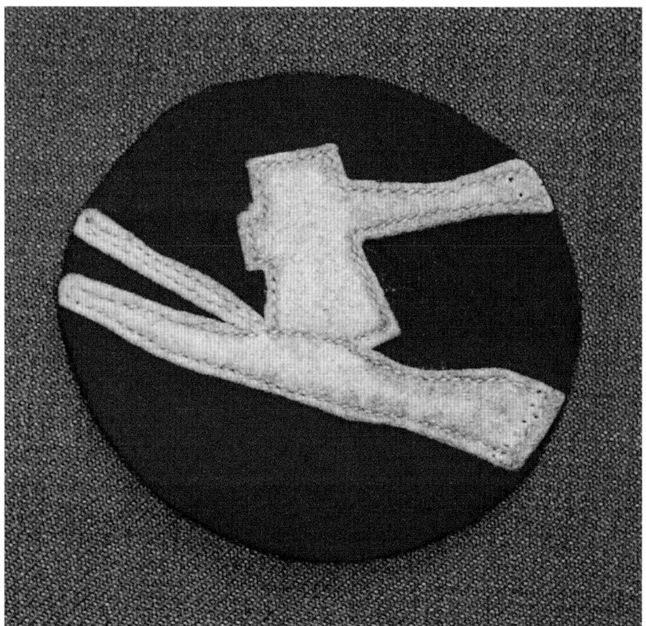

Fig. 84.7. Interwar. Felt on felt.

Fig. 84.8. World War II/Post World War II. FE. Comparison on U.S. made patches, top, and a German made patch, bottom.

Figs. 84.9 to 84.11. Above and below left: Period Unknown. U.S. made patch, exact use unknown. During the construction of this book three different examples were encountered. All were worn and showed some use. The construction style would suggest they date from immediately before World War II to just after. It has been suggested that this patch was used by the 84th Division's Military Police Platoon, but this theory is unconfirmed.

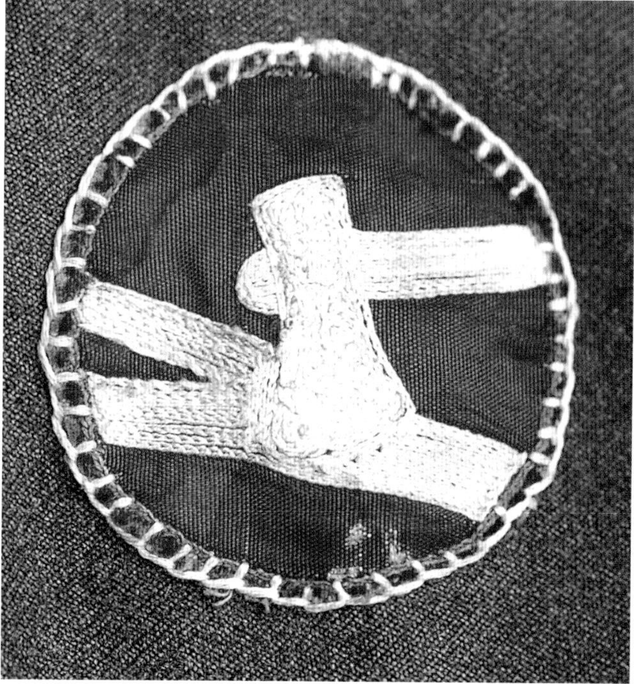

Fig. 84.12. Post World War II, Germany. CS on satin.

Fig. 84.13. Post World War II, Germany. Part CS, part ME on cotton.

Fig. 84.14. Post World War II, Germany. Bullion cord on felt with HE border.

Fig. 84.15. Post World War II, Germany. Bullion on felt with HE and bullion border.

Fig. 84.16. Post World War II, Germany. Bullion on felt.

Fig. 84.17. Post World War II, Germany. Bullion cord on felt applied to a wool base.

Fig. 84.18. Post World War II, Germany. U.S. made FE patch with ME on cotton "Railsplitters" nickname tab. During World War II the division was known as the "Railsplitters" an extension of the World War I "Lincoln" moniker.

Fig. 84.19. Post World War II, Germany. ME on cotton nickname tab attached to a U.S. made patch with a German added ME white border.

Fig. 84.20. Post World War II, Germany. ME on cotton "Railsplitter" nickname tab with a bullion on wool patch.

Fig. 84.21. Post World War II, Germany. Bullion on wool patch and tab.

Fig. 84.22. Post World War II, Germany. ME on felt tab with bullion on felt patch.

Figs. 84.23 and 84.24. Post World War II. FE. These two examples show the types of tabs worn by the 84th Division during the time it was an Airborne Division – September 24, 1947 - March 1, 1952. ***Fig. 84.24*** was worn by a soldier in the 333rd Airborne Infantry Regiment.

Fig. 84.25. Post World War II, Korea. ME on satin like cloth.

84TH U.S. INFANTRY "RAILSPLITTER" DIVISION

TO THE OFFICERS AND MEN OF THE 183RD AND 59TH VOLKSGRENADIER DIVISIONS

We have known each other for a long time. We got acquainted back at Geilenkirchen, Prummern, Würm, Süggerath and Müllendorf. At that time we mauled the 183rd Volksgrenadier Division so badly that it had to be entirely regrouped. The 10th ϟϟ Panzer Division, the 9th Panzer Division, and the 15th Panzer Grenadier Division had to come to your aid. Nevertheless, we broke through those four divisions and the Westwall and pushed to the Roer. Nevertheless, the whole 1st Bn of the 343rd Rgt was either captured or killed in Würm. The Battalion Commander Capt Otten wrote, in a letter now in our possession, that he was waiting in an Officers Replacement Pool to take command of an entirely new battalion. That was just a beginning. The same fate awaits any other unit opposing the 84th U.S. Infantry Division.

We were instrumental in stopping Manteuffel's 5th and Dietrich's 6th Panzer Armies in the Ardennes, and then we threw them in retreat across the Our River. And our losses were very light. The combat strength of our companies is over 200 men. Yours is 50-70 men. (Let your G-2 take note of that).

The following German divisions felt the might of our blows in the Geilenkirchen Sector:

183 V G Div
15 Pz Gren Div
9 Pz Div
10 ϟϟ Pz Div

And from von Rundstedt's luckless adventure in the Ardennes, these units will always remember us:

560 V G Div
116 Pz Div
2 ϟϟ Pz Div
9 Pz Div
9 ϟϟ Pz Div
130 Pz LEHR Div

Thousands of German officers and enlisted men have made a wise choice. They have surrendered to the 84th Infantry Division. Many more thousands were not so wise. They are dead.

WHAT WILL YOUR CHOICE BE?

German prisoners-of-war are fairly treated by us. Approach our outposts unarmed. Web belt and helmet off. Hands over your head. The password: "EI SÖRRENDER" (I surrender).

"THE RAILSPLITTERS"
(84 U.S. INFANTRY DIVISION)

BETTER BE CAPTURED THAN KILLED

CPH · BOe

Figs. 84.26 and 84.27. World War II. Front and back of a translated surrender leaflet of the type dropped on the Germans by the 84th division.

Fig. 84.28. Left: Post World War II, Germany. 84th Division side of the football program for a game between the "Railsplitters" and the 101st Airborne Division.

Fig. 84.29. Post World War II, Germany. Engraved plastic souvenir coasters and letter opener from Heidelberg.

Fig. 85.1. World War I. Unidentified Artilleryman from the 85th Division wearing a ME on wool patch.

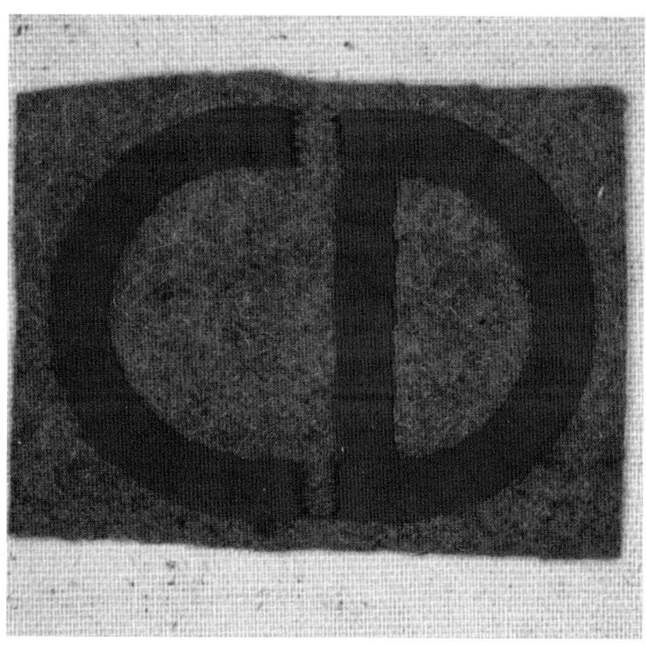

Fig. 85.2. World War I. ME on wool of the same style being worn in ***Fig. 85.1***.

Fig. 85.3. World War I. ME on felt.

Fig. 85.4. World War I. ME on wool.

Fig. 85.5. World War I. Wool on wool.

Fig. 85.6. World War II. Five different FE patches.

Figs. 85.7 and 85.8. World War II, Italy. HE on cotton.

Figs. 85.9 and 85.10. World War II, Italy. Front and back of a woven style patch.

Fig. 85.11. World War II, Italy. HE on suede with bullion border patch and a bullion on suede with HE border "Custer Division" nickname tab.

Fig. 85.12. World War II, Germany. ME on wool.

Fig. 85.13. World War II, Germany. HE on felt with bullion detail and border.

Fig. 85.14. Period Unknown. ME on felt miniature patch.

Fig. 86.1. World War I. Wool on wool with HE lettering.

Fig. 86.2. World War I. ME on felt.

Fig. 86.3. World War I. HE on wool.

Fig. 86.4. World War I. HE silk on wool.

Fig. 86.5. World War I. Felt on felt with embroidered lettering.

Figs. 86.6 to 86.8. Above and two below: Interwar. ME on felt.

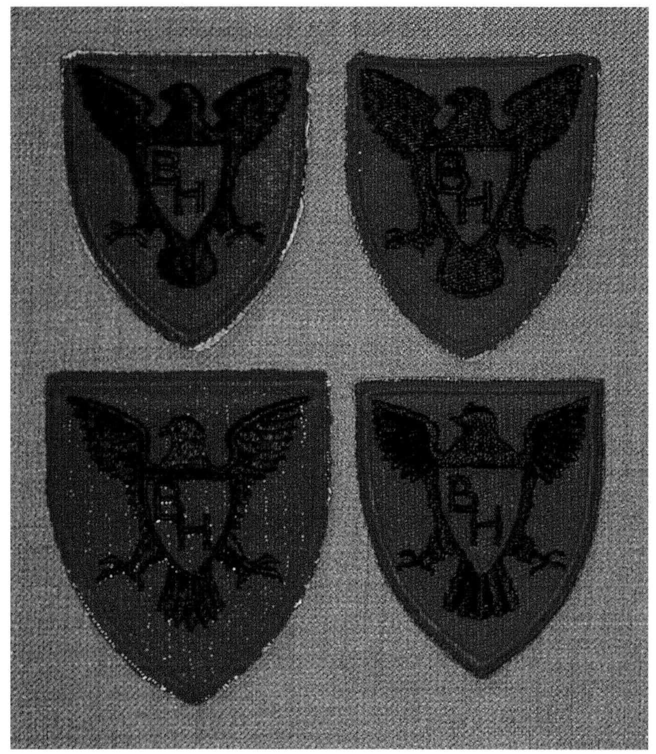

Fig. 86.9. World War II/Post World War II. FE. Comparison of U.S. made patches and a German made, bottom right.

Fig. 86.10. Post World War II, Germany. FE.

Fig. 86.11. Post World War II, Germany. HE on felt and wool with cello border.

Fig. 86.12. Post World War II, Germany. HE on felt with red bullion border. Note that this is a right facing Blackhawk.

Fig. 86.13. Post World War II, Japan. FE silk.

Fig. 86.14. Post World War II, Germany? Plastic patch type DI.

Fig. 86.15. World War II/Post World War II, Philippines. The 86th Division was one of two Army divisions to have service in the European and Pacific Theaters, the other being the 97th Division. This pin commemorates that distinction. Occasionally this pin can be found with a painted background.

Fig. 87.1. World War I. Pair of unidentified doughboys, one wearing an 87th Division patch.

Fig. 87.2. World War I. Wool on wool with a soutache divide on the acorn.

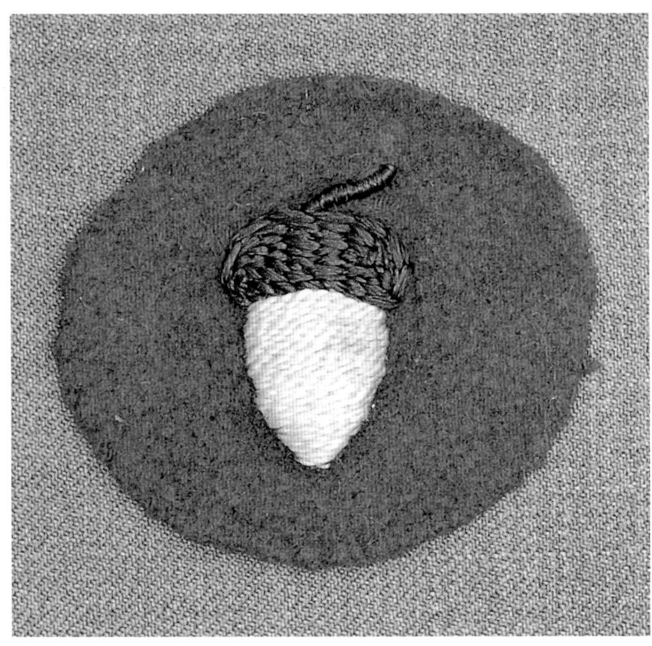

Figs. 87.3 to 87.5. Above and two below: World War I. HE on wool.

Fig. 87.6. World War I. Liberty Loan.

Figs. 87.7 and 87.8. Above and below: World War I. ME on felt. It is believed that patches with a red background and leaf are for the division artillery regiments.

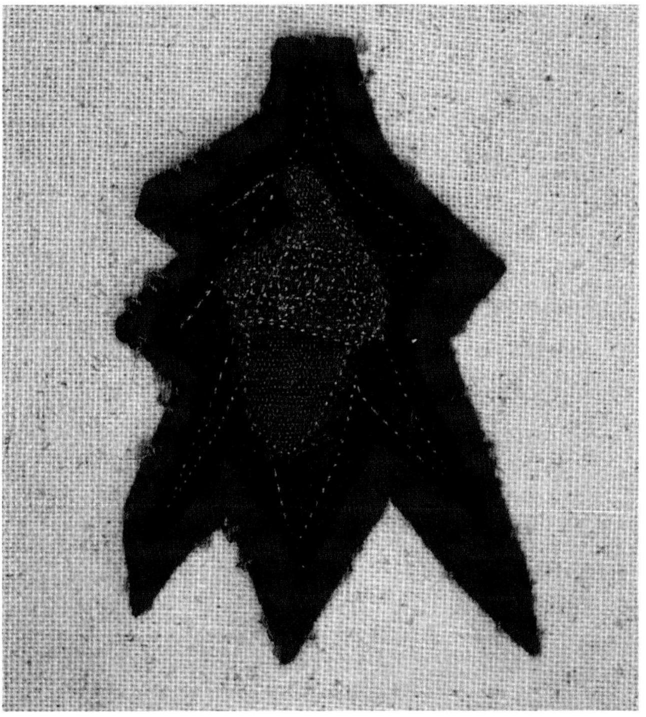

Fig. 87.9. World War I. Wool on felt.

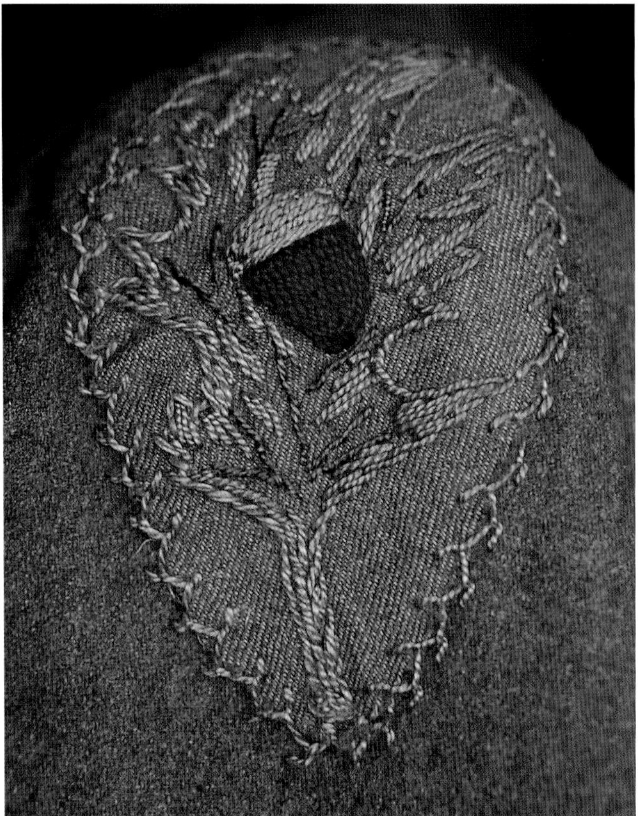

Fig. 87.10. World War I. Pfc. William A. Fritz. Pfc. Fritz was with one of the division's Artillery Regiments. HE on wool.

Fig. 87.11. Interwar. ME on felt.

Fig. 87.12. Interwar. ME on wool.

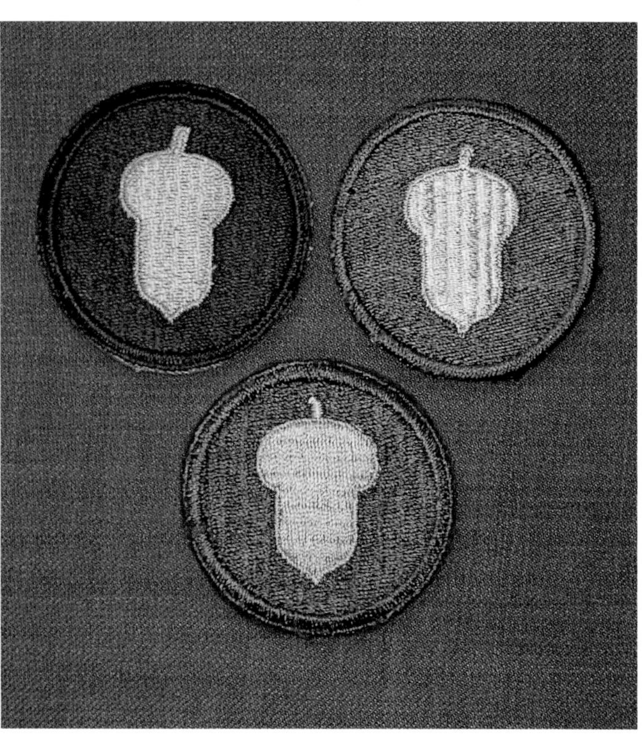

Fig. 87.13. World War II. Three different U.S. made FE patches. Of note is the bottom example with an opposite direction acorn stem.

Fig. 87.14. World War II, England. FE, ODB.

Fig. 87.15. Post World War II, Germany. FE.

Fig. 87.16. Post World War II, Germany. Cello cord on felt.

Fig. 88.1. World War I. Unidentified 88th Division Engineer wearing a simple cut out patch. During World War I the 88th Division occasionally used a colored cloverleaf to designate different units within the division. Blue for infantry, red for artillery, purple for machine gun battalions and black for engineers.

Fig. 88.2. World War I. ME on felt

Fig. 88.3. World War I. Wool applied over dark blue velvet.

Fig. 88.4. World War I. Wool applied over burgundy velvet, presumably for wear by artillery units.

Fig. 88.5. World War I. Black cloverleaf on wool base.

Fig. 88.6. World War II. FE, ODB.

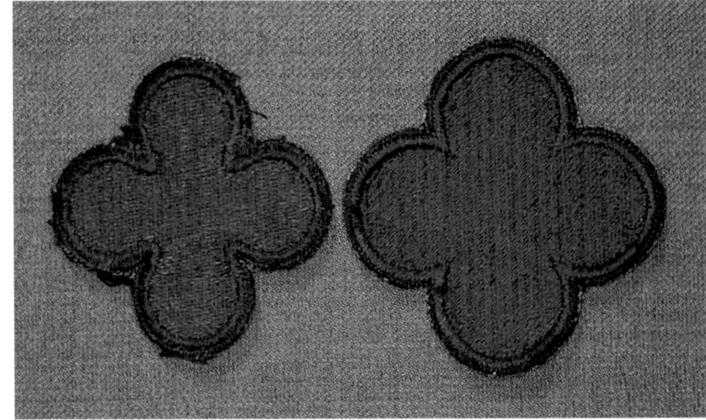

Fig. 88.7. World War II. Two different U.S. made FE patches.

Fig. 88.9. World War II. FE with added white cord border.

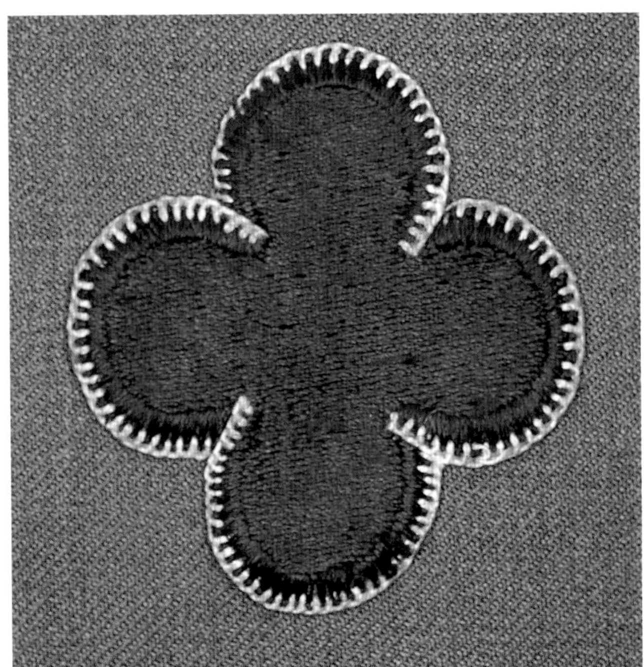

Fig. 88.8. World War II. U.S. made FE patch with added white border.

Fig. 88.10. Right: World War II. FE with added red border. During World War II, red was added to distinguish the artillery units within the division.

Fig. 88.11. World War II. FE, with added red artillery garrison cap piping.

Fig. 88.12. World War II. FE with added red border and "Blue Devil" nickname. During World War II the division was known as the "Blue Devil" division or the "Blue Devils"

Fig. 88.13. World War II, Italy. ME on wool.

Fig. 88.14. World War II, Italy. HE on satin.

Fig. 88.15. World War II, Italy. HE on wool.

Fig. 88.16. World War II, Italy. HE on wool with red artillery garrison cap piping.

Figs. 88.17 and 88.18. World War II, Italy. Woven.

Fig. 88.19. World War II, Italy. Woven with added medical garrison cap piping.

Fig. 88.20. World War II, Italy. Bullion on woven cloth background.

Fig. 88.21. World War II, Italy. HE on satin patch and tab.

Fig. 88.22. World War II, Italy. ME on satin patch and tab.

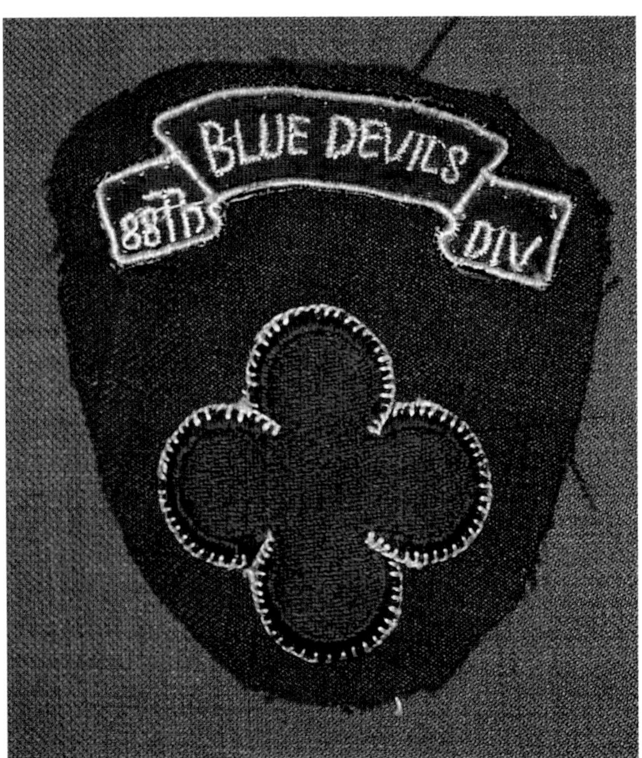

Fig. 88.23. World War II, Italy. U.S. made patch with added border and ME on satin tab.

Fig. 88.24. World War II, Italy. Woven patch with HE on satin tab.

Fig. 88.25. World War II, Italy. U.S. made patch with added artillery garrison cap piping and HE on wool tab.

Figs. 88.26 and 88.27. World War II, Italy. Bullion on wool patch and tab.

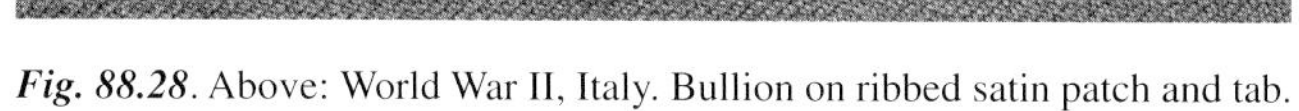

Fig. 88.28. Above: World War II, Italy. Bullion on ribbed satin patch and tab.

Fig. 88.29. Above right: World War II, Italy. Sgt. Willard Wachter, 351st Infantry Regiment. Bullion on felt. Of special note is the arrow configuration of the "88" side of the tab.

Fig. 88.30. Right: World War II, Italy. Bullion on satin patch applied to a wool base and a bullion on satin "Italy" tab with HE border.

Fig. 88.31. World War II, Italy. 2nd Lt. James Masson, 337th Field Artillery Battalion. Lt. Masson won a Silver and Bronze Star and was a recipient of a battlefield commission, going from Private to 2nd Lieutenant. Bullion on satin or silk background with HE border.

Fig. 88.32. World War II, Italy. ME on satin. Of special note is the "Blue Devil" likeness at the center of the patch and the addition of "Italy" to the tab.

Fig. 88.33. World War II, Italy. ME on felt patch and tab.

Fig. 88.34. World War II, Italy. HE on wool with bullion border patch and bullion on wool tab.

Fig. 88.35. World War II, Italy. Bullion on wool with HE details patch and ME on ribbed satin tab.

Figs. 88.36 to 88.38. Above and two below: World War II, Italy. Bullion on wool with HE detail patch and bullion on wool tab. ***Fig. 88.36*** Courtesy of Peter M. Bennethum.

Fig. 88.39. World War II, Italy. Bullion on wool with HE details.

Fig. 88.42. World War II, Italy. Bullion on satin.

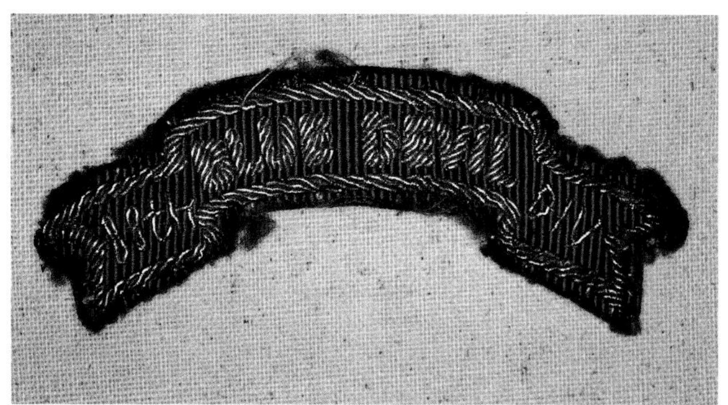

Fig. 88.44. World War II, Italy. Bullion on ribbed satin background.

Fig. 88.40. World War II, Italy. ME on wool.

Fig. 88.41. World War II, Italy. HE on satin.

Fig. 88.43. World War II, Italy. ME on wool with a red cord border.

Fig. 88.45. World War II, Italy. Bullion on satin applied to a twill base.

Fig. 88.46. Post World War II, Germany. ME on felt.

Fig. 88.47. Post World War II, TM. ME with white border.

Fig. 88.48. Post World War II, Germany. FE.

Fig. 88.49. Post World War II, Germany. Woven.

Fig. 88/50. Post World War II, Germany. HE on twill with bullion border.

Fig. 88.51. World War II, Italy. 351st Infantry Regiment bullion on wool DI.

Fig. 88.52. World War II, Italy. 351st Infantry Regt. souvenir belt buckle.

Fig. 89.1. World War I. Group of musicians from the 354th Infantry Regiment. Of special note is the 89th Division insignia painted on the guard house in the background. During World War I the 89th Division used an extensive range of colors or color combinations at the center of the patch to designate different units within the division. The colors used by the 89th are as follows: Sky Blue – 177th Infantry Brigade, Navy Blue – 178th Infantry Brigade, Scarlet – 164th Field Artillery Brigade, Scarlet and Orange – 340th Machine Gun Battalion, Scarlet and Sky Blue – 341st Machine Gun Battalion, Scarlet and Navy Blue – 342nd Machine Gun Battalion, Scarlet piped with White – 314th Engineer Regiment, Orange – 314th Signal Battalion, Purple piped with White – Supply Train, White with a Red Cross – Sanitary Train, No Color – Division Headquarters.

Fig. 89.2. World War I. HE on wool. This particular style of patch is the basis for many of the different color variations that can be found.

Fig. 89.3. World War I. 177th Infantry Brigade. The color section of this example is a faded sky blue. HE on wool.

Fig. 89.4. World War I. 177th Infantry Brigade. ME on wool.

Fig. 89.5. World War I. 177th Infantry Brigade. Stencil on wool. While not definitely a patch, this may be a souvenir made with either a helmet or equipment stencil.

Fig. 89.6. World War I. Unidentified musician from either the 177th or 178th Infantry Brigade.

Fig. 89.8. World War I. 178th Infantry Brigade. Wool on wool. This "skeleton" design can often be found on a souvenir pillow cover.

Fig. 89.7. World War I. 178th Infantry Brigade. HE on wool with applied felt center section.

Fig. 89.9. World War I. A group of 89th Division officers receiving awards from General Pershing. Visible in the photo are several variations of shoulder patches and the division insignia painted on helmets. The photo is significant in that it shows another color coded system used by the division. The medical officer, second from right, displays a Best Regiment in Brigade color panel. When filled in with white the four panels around the center section were awards for proficiency in drill and inspection. Each of the four panels had a different significance. From lower left moving clockwise: Panel 1 Best Company or Battery in the Battalion, Panel 2 Best Battalion in the Regiment, Panel 3 Best Regiment in the Brigade, and Panel 4 Best Brigade in the Division.

Fig. 89.10. World War I. 178th Infantry Brigade with Best Regiment in the Brigade and Best Brigade in the Division Awards. ME on felt with HE award sections.

Fig. 89.11. World War I. 178th Infantry Brigade with Best Company in the Battalion and Best Brigade in the Division awards. The sunflower is a symbol of Kansas, the home state of the 353rd Infantry Regiment . Wool on wool with satin center section and HE award sections.

Fig. 89.12. Left: World War I. Unidentified 89th Division Doughboys, possibly from one of the Infantry Brigades, with Best Regiment in the Brigade and Best Brigade in the Division awards.

Fig. 89.13. World War I. 164th Field Artillery Brigade. HE on wool.

Fig. 89.14. World War I. 164th Field Artillery Brigade with Best Battalion in Regiment award. HE on wool.

Fig. 89.15. World War I. 341st Artillery Regiment with Best Battalion in Regiment award. HE on wool with CS center and award sections.

Fig. 89.16. Left: World War I. Cover of the 341st Field Artillery Regiment's history. Sources such as this are invaluable in identifying some of the more obscure insignia that can be found. The "C" in the center section has usually been interpreted as standing for Colorado, the state from which the unit drew the majority of its personal. Another plausible explanation is that the Governor of the State of Colorado presented the unit with its colors in a ceremony before departing to join the rest of the division and this is the reason for the "C". Still another possibility is that it stands for battery "C", which fired the first shot of the Regiment in France, saw more action than any other battery, suffered the first death in the Regiment and the most casualties.

Fig. 89.17. World War I. 340th Machine Gun Battalion with Best Company in the Battalion and Best Regiment in the Brigade awards. This insignia has long been misidentified as the 343rd Machine Gun Battalion, but in fact that unit was assigned to the 90th Division.

Fig. 89.18. World War I. 341st Machine Gun Battalion being worn beneath a District of Paris patch. Wool on wool with a HE color section. Bullion on wool District of Paris.

Fig. 89.19. World War I. 341st Machine Gun Battalion. ME on wool.

Fig. 89.20. World War I. 314th Engineer Regiment. The red has faded somewhat and the color from the "W" has bled into the white border. Felt on wool with ME over satin center section.

Fig. 89.21. World War I. Supply Train. Felt on wool with purple silk center (unfortunately missing) and soutache border.

Fig. 89.22. World War I. Supply Train. Wool on wool with velvet center section and bullion border.

Fig. 89.23. World War I. Sanitary Train. Wool on wool with a HE red cross.

Fig. 89.24. World War I/Interwar. 177th Infantry Brigade. Wool on wool with ME color section.

Fig. 89.25. World War I/Interwar. 164th Field Artillery Brigade. Wool on wool with ME color section.

Fig. 89.26. World War II. Two different FE patches.

Fig. 89.27. World War II/Post World War II. Comparison of U.S. made patch, left, and a German made, right.

Fig. 89.28. Post World War II, Germany. HE on a tapestry background with a cello border on a wool base.

Fig. 89.29. Post World War II, Germany. HE on felt with bullion detail.

Fig. 89.30. Post World War II, Germany. HE on wool with a bullion border.

Fig. 89.31. Post World War II. FE. Some time after World War II the Division switched to a red, white and blue color scheme.

Fig. 89.32. Post World War II. ME on twill.

Fig. 90.1. World War I. Two unidentified doughboys wearing 90th Division patches without the normal background shield.

Fig. 90.2. World War I. Wool on wool.

Fig. 90.3. World War I. HE on wool.

Fig. 90.4. World War I. HE on wool. Black monogram variation.

Fig. 90.5. World War I. Unusual needle point variation.

Fig. 90.6. World War I. Jack and Bill Barber. Bill is wearing a ME on wool or felt style patch.

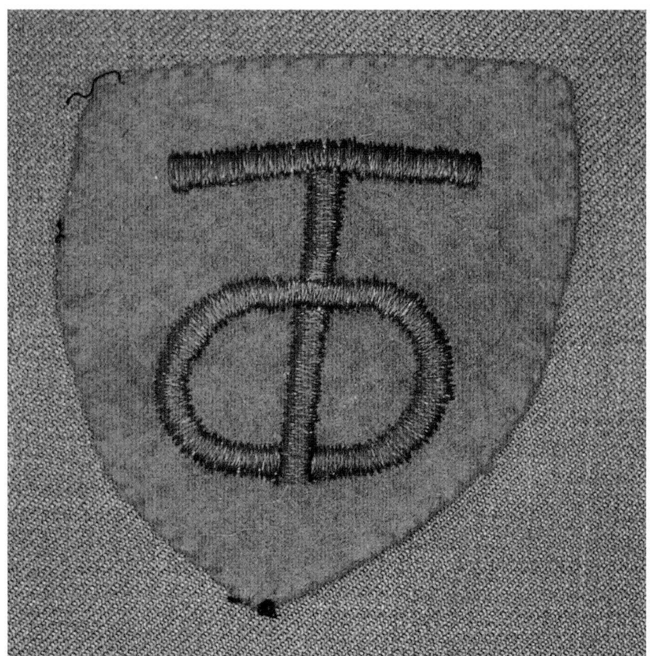

Figs. 90.7 and 90.8. Above and below: World War I. ME on felt.

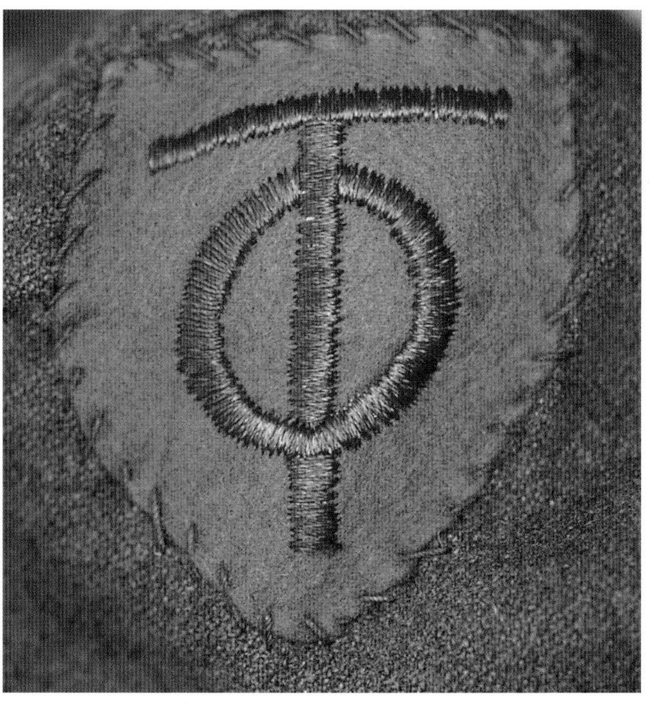

Fig. 90.9. Left: World War I. HE on wool.

Fig. 90.10. Interwar. ME on felt.

Fig. 90.11. Interwar. ME on wool.

Fig. 90.12. Interwar. ME on wool.

Fig. 90.13. Interwar. ME on officer's dark OD wool elastique.

Fig. 90.14. World War II. Three different U.S. made FE patches. Of note is the bottom example with rounded lower corners.

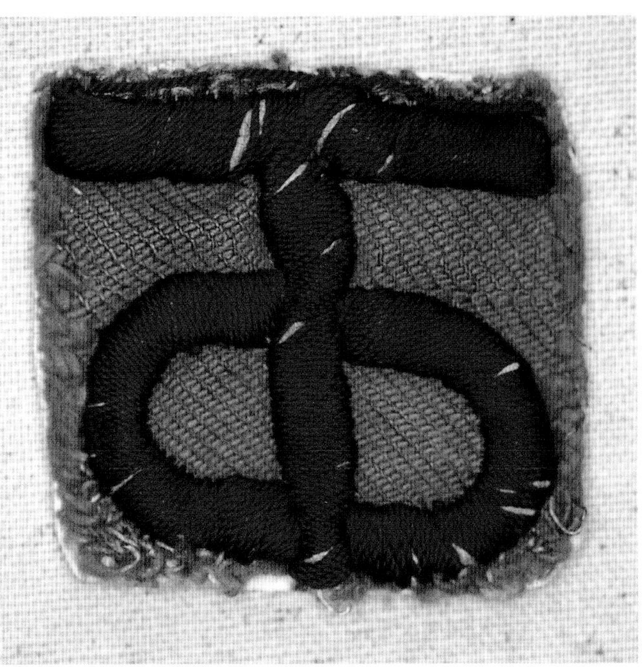

Fig. 90.15. Post World War II, Germany. HE on twill.

Fig. 90.16. Post World War II, Germany. HE on wool.

Fig. 90.17. Post World War II, Germany. HE on tapestry background with a cello border on a wool base.

Fig. 90.18. Post World War II, Germany. HE on wool with bullion border.

Fig. 90.19. Post World War II, Germany. HE on felt with bullion detail and border.

Fig. 91.1. World War I. Sgt. Roy N. Clark, Co. E, 316th Ammo Train. Simple felt cut out.

Fig. 91.2. World War I. Interesting "trench art" from the lining of Sgt. Clark's jacket showing a doughboy seated on a large artillery shell.

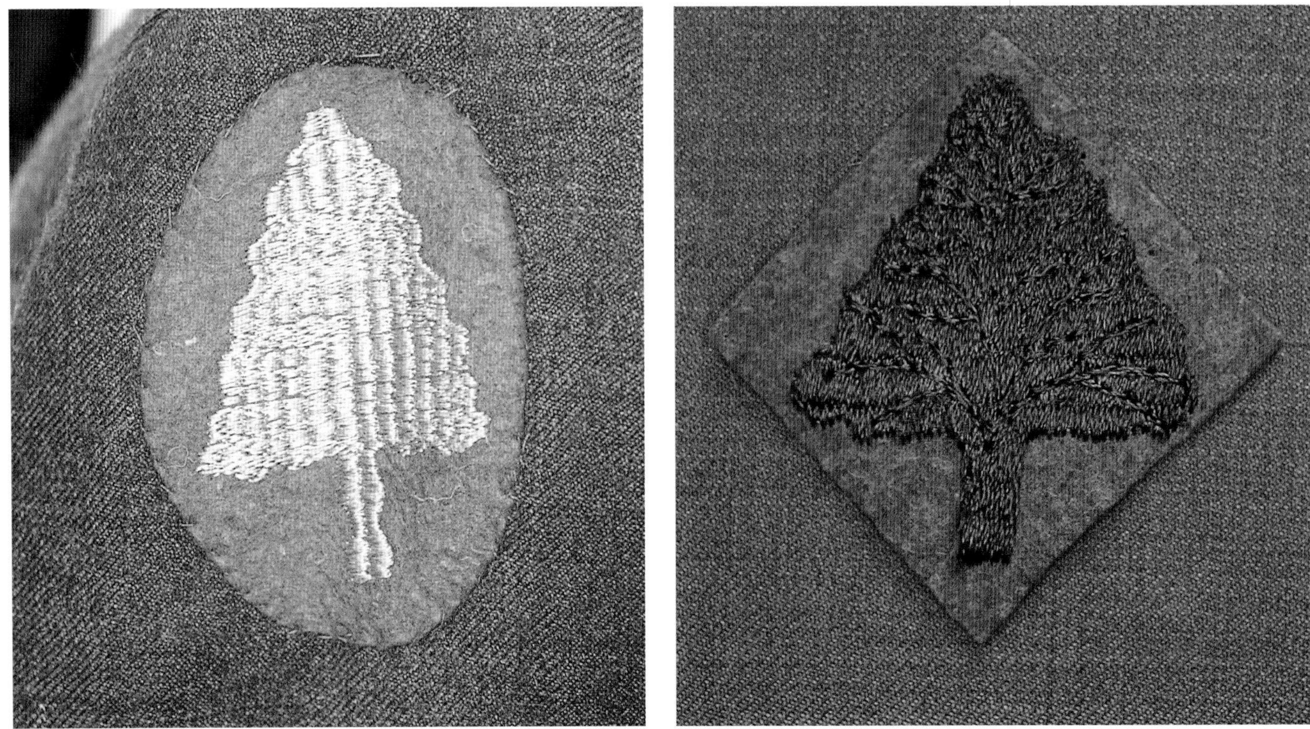

Figs. 91.3 and 91.4. World War I. ME on felt.

Figs. 91.5 and 91.6. World War I. ME on wool

Fig. 91.7. World War I/Interwar. Me on wool.

Fig. 91.8. World War I. Very nice example of a 91st Division insignia directly embroidered to the sleeve of a uniform with the division's numerical designation.

Fig. 91.9. World War I. Liberty Loan. During World War I the 91st was more commonly referred to as the "Evergreen Division". This alternate design features the division's numerical designation and the letters "WW", which stand for "Wild West".

Fig. 91.10. World War I. ME on felt

Fig. 91.11. World War II. FE.

Fig. 91.12. World War II. FE patch added to a white felt background.

Fig. 91.13. World War II. FE. This example features a straight border instead of a contoured one.

Fig. 91.15. World War II. FE, ODB.

Fig. 91.14. Left: World War II. FE. Two patches from the same manufacturer, one with an ODB.

Fig. 91.16. World War II. FE with a white border.

Figs. 91.17 and 91.18. Above and below: World War II, Italy. Two different woven patches.

Fig. 91.19. World War II, Italy. HE.

Fig. 91.20. World War II, Italy. Twill pine tree on a wool base with bullion detail and border and a bullion on wool tab.

Fig. 91.21. World War II, Italy. FE, ODB U.S. made patch with an Italian made ME on satin like cloth with a HE border tab. During World War II the Division's nickname was "Powder River".

Fig. 91.22. Post World War II, Germany. FE, ODB.

Fig. 92.1. World War I. Unidentified member of the 92nd Division wearing an applied construction style patch. Like other divisions during World War I, the 92nd also used different background colors to designate different units within the division. Blue was used for infantry, red for artillery and trench mortar, buff for quartermaster and green for sanitary train.

Fig. 92.2. World War I. 92nd Division Artillery. Felt on felt.

Fig. 92.3. World War I. 92nd Division Artillery. ME on felt

Fig. 92.4. World War I. 92nd Division Infantry. Liberty Loan.

Fig. 92.5. World War II. Four different U.S. made FE patches. As with the OD border patch shown in ***Fig. 81.19***, the OD border example at bottom right is also believed to be Post World War II, as it is manufactured in the same manner.

Fig. 92.6. World War II. U.S. made FE patch with Artillery Garrison Cap piping added to the border.

Fig. 92.7. World War II, Italy. Woven.

Fig. 92.8. World War II, Italy. Woven with added Infantry Garrison Cap piping.

Fig. 92.9. World War II, Italy. HE on wool.

Fig. 92.10. World War II, Italy. HE on wool with bullion border.

Fig. 92.11. World War II, Germany. HE on tapestry like background on a wool base.

Fig. 93.1. World War I. Felt on felt.

Fig. 93.2. Interwar. Wool on felt background.

Fig. 93.3. World War II. FE.

Fig. 93.4. Post World War II, Germany. HE on felt with a bullion border.

Fig. 93.5. Post World War II, Germany. Bullion cord on felt on a wool base.

Figs. 94.1 and 94.2. Interwar. ME on felt. Prior to September 5, 1942 the 94th Division utilized a pilgrim design as its insignia. After this date the division switched to the more familiar "94" numerical design.

Fig. 94.3. Interwar. ME on wool

Fig. 94.4. World War II. Two different FE, ODB pilgrim patches.

Fig. 94.5. Right: Interwar/World War II. ME on twill.

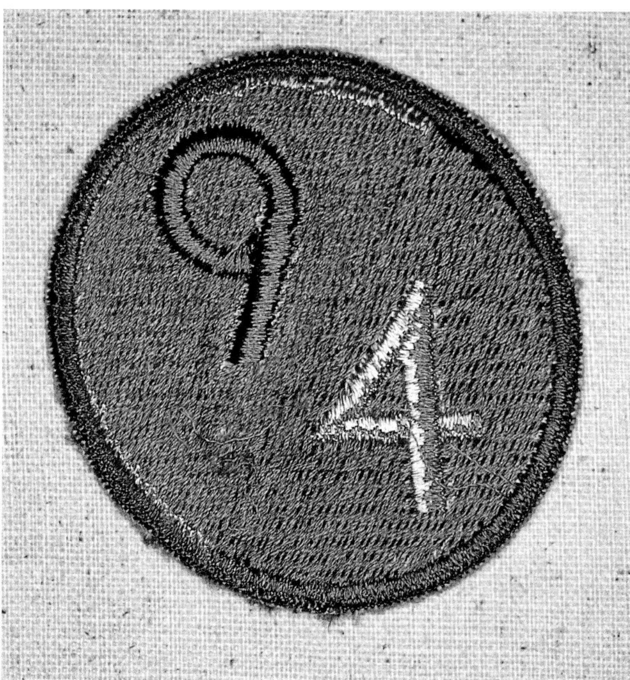

Fig. 94.6 and 94.7. World War II. Front and back of a patch from possibly the first run of the "94" design. The embroidery pattern and size is identical to ***Fig. 94.5***.

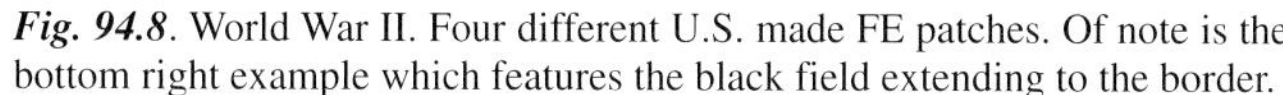

Fig. 94.8. World War II. Four different U.S. made FE patches. Of note is the bottom right example which features the black field extending to the border.

Fig. 94.9. Post World War II, Germany. FE. In this variation blue is substituted for black.

Fig. 94.10. Post World War II, Germany. HE on twill.

Fig. 94.11. Post World War II, Germany. HE on felt with cello border on a wool base. With this patch and ***Fig. 94.9*** it is unclear if the color substitutions were intended to designate different units within the division.

Fig. 94.12. Post World War II, Germany. ME on satin with bullion border detail.

Fig. 94.13. Post World War II, Germany. HE on felt with bullion detail and border.

Fig. 94.14. Post World War II, Germany. HE on a satin ribbon background with bullion detail and border on a wool base.

Fig. 94.15. Post World War II, Czechoslovakia. A nice example of folk art commemorating the 94th Division's time spent in Strakonice.

Fig. 94.16. Post World War II. Sometime after World War II the 94th Division returned to using the pilgrim design. The two main differences between the World War II and the Post War versions are the border colors, OD vs. black respectively, and the diameter, the Post War patch being smaller. FE.

Fig. 95.1. World War II. 95th Division Musician and his sweetheart.

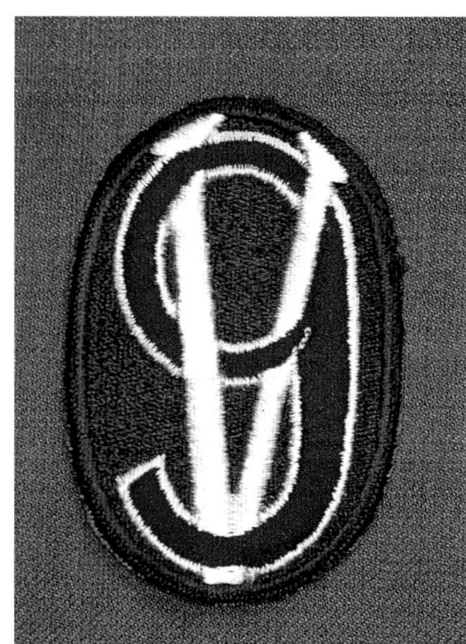

Fig. 95.2. World War II. FE, ODB.

Figs. 95.3 and 95.4. World War II. FE.

Fig. 95.5. World War II. FE. This example features a thin monogram and a "9" without a white outline.

Fig. 95.6. World War II. FE. In this example the "9" is again without an outline and the left arm of the "V" overlays the "9" at the top.

Fig. 96.1. World War II. Unidentified 96th Division GI from the 383rd Infantry Regiment wearing a FE patch.

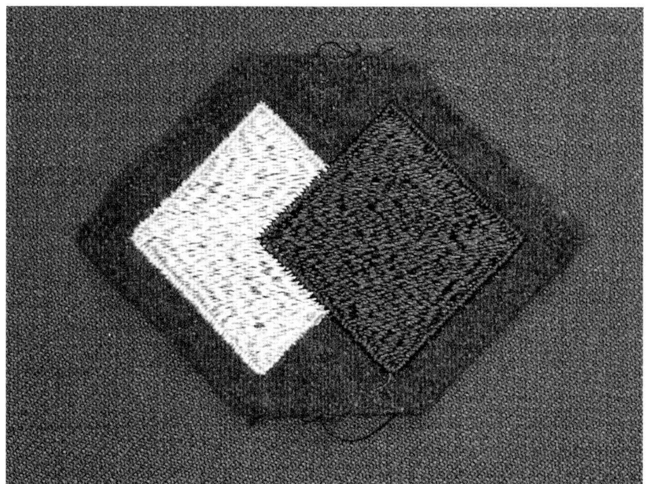

Fig. 96.2. Interwar. ME on wool.

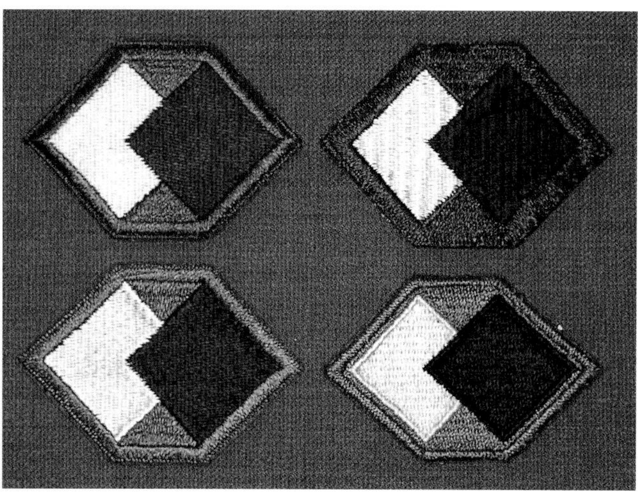

Fig. 96.3. World War II. Four different U.S. made FE patches.

Fig. 96.4. Post World War II, Germany. HE and bullion on wool.

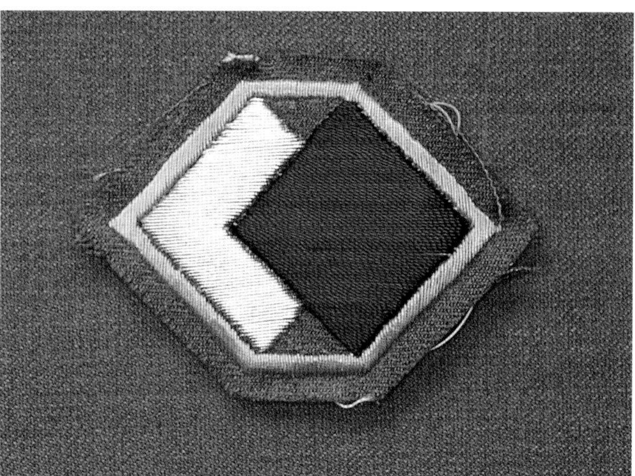

Fig. 96.5. Post World War II, Germany. HE and bullion on wool with a cello border.

Fig. 96.6. World War II/Post World War II, Philippines. Painted patch type pin with "Dead Eyes" unit nickname and Leyte and Okinawa campaign ribbon.

Figs. 97.1 and 97.2. Interwar. ME on wool.

Figs. 97.3 and 97.4. Post World War II, Germany. Bullion on felt.

Fig. 97.5. Post World War II, Japan. FE.

Fig. 97.6. Post World War II, Japan. Oversized 97th Division patch. ME on a souvenir handkerchief.

Fig. 98.1. Post World War II, Japan. 98th Division souvenir painted on a Japanese flag. The 98th Division was the only World War II U.S. Division not to participate in combat. At the time of the Japanese surrender the 98th was in training for the proposed invasion of Japan. After the end of the war the Division was part of the occupation forces.

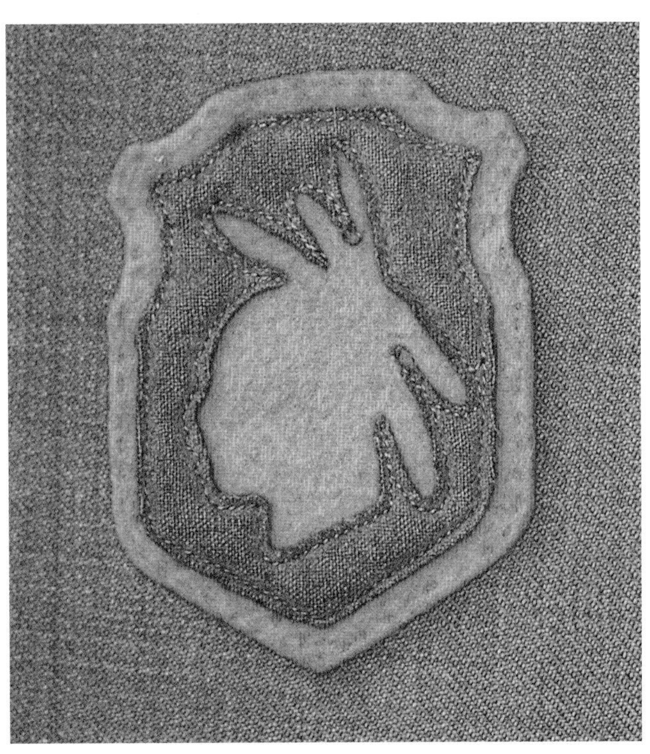

Fig. 98.2. Interwar. Wool on felt.

Figs. 98.3 to 98.5. Above and two below: World War II. FE. Six examples showing the wide range of color, from dark orange to golden yellow, that the 98th Division can be found in.

Fig. 98.6. Post World War II, Japan. FE silk.

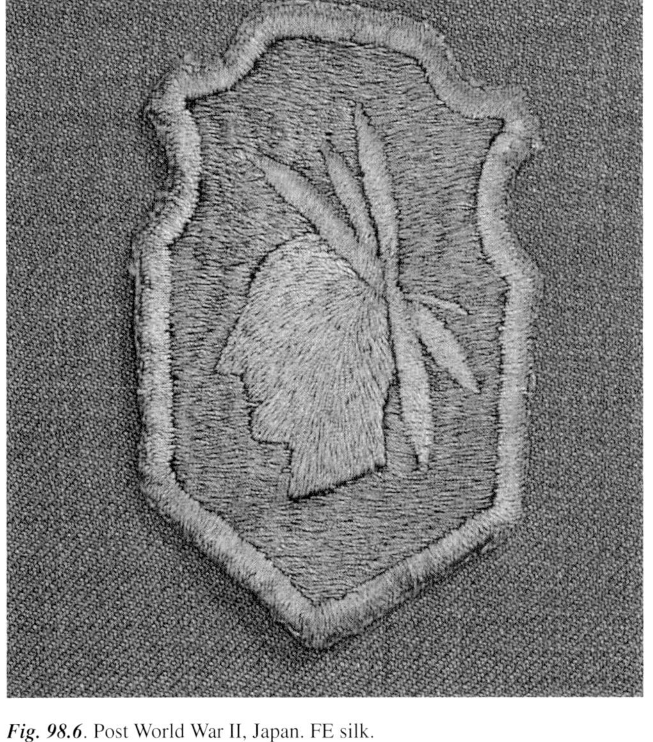

Fig. 98.7. Post World War II, Japan. Bullion on silk.

Fig. 98.8. Post World War II, Japan. HE silk handkerchief.

Fig. 98.9. Right: Post World War II, Japan. HE silk wallet.

Figs. 98.10 and 98.11. Post World War II, Germany. HE on felt

Fig. 98.12. Post World War II, Germany. HE on felt on a wool base.

Fig. 99.1. Interwar. HE checkerboard with felt shield on a wool base still attached to a shirt remnant.

Fig. 99.2. Interwar. ME on wool.

Figs. 99.3 and 99.4. World War II. Front and back of four different U.S. made FE patches. Of note is the reversed checkerboard pattern of the upper right example.

Fig. 99.5. World War II. Reversed checkerboard with added Infantry garrison cap piping.

Fig. 99.6. World War II. FE, black border variation.

Fig. 99.7. World War II, England. FE.

Figs. 99.8 and 99.9. Post World War II, Germany. FE.

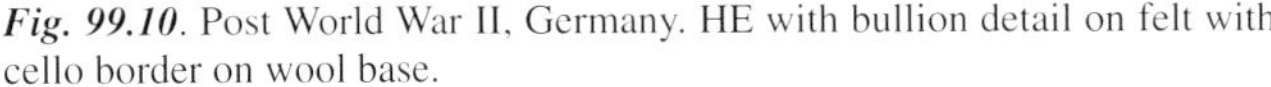

Fig. 99.10. Post World War II, Germany. HE with bullion detail on felt with cello border on wool base.

Fig. 99.11. Post World War II, Germany. HE on felt with soutache border.

Fig. 99.12. Post World War II, Germany. HE on wool with bullion detail and HE border.

Fig. 99.13. Post World War II, Germany. HE on wool with bullion detail and HE border patch with integral "Battle Babies" nickname tab.

Fig. 100.1. World War II. FE.

Fig. 100.2. World War II. FE. Reversed color variant with gold on the top of the numerals.

Fig. 100.3. World War II. ME on satin souvenir patch.

Fig. 100.4. Post World War II, Germany. Front and back of a FE German made patch.

Fig. 100.5. Post World War II, Germany. HE on wool.

Fig. 100.6. Post World War II, Germany. HE on felt with cello detail and border on a wool base.

Fig. 100.7. Right: Post World War II, Germany. Bullion on satin with a corded border.

Fig. 100.8. Post World War II, Germany. Front and back of a bullion and cello cording on felt with bullion border patch.

Fig. 100.9. Post World War II, Germany. Bullion on felt with a bullion inner border.

Fig. 100.10. Post World War II, Germany. Bullion cord on felt with a bullion border.

Fig. 100.11. Post World War II, Germany. Bullion on felt with bullion border and integral "Century" and "Sons of Bitche" tabs. "Century" is the division's nickname while "Sons of Bitche" is an unofficial honorary title earned by members of the division who participated in a hard fought series of battles near the town of Bitche, France.

Figs. 100.12 and 100.13. Front and back of a membership card for The Society of the Sons of Bitche.

Fig. 101.1. World War II. Pvt. Jack Higgins and his bride.

Fig. 101.2. Interwar. HE on wool. During the interwar period the 101st Division was a non-airborne division with different organizational components than in World War II.

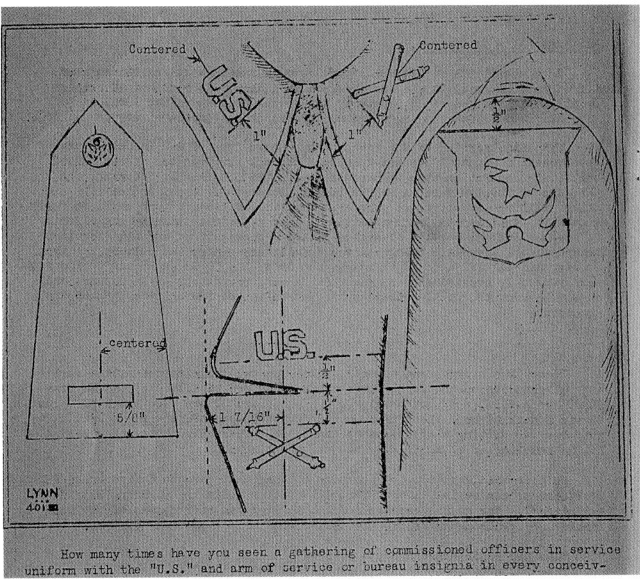

Fig. 101.3. Interwar. Page from the May/June 1938 issue of the *Iron Division Bulletin* showing the prescribed wear of a commissioned officer's insignia including the early style shoulder patch.

Fig. 101.4. World War II. FE, ODB.

Fig. 101.5. World War II. FE. Note how this patch and *Fig. 101.4* are embroidered in similar fashion.

Fig. 101.6. World War II. FE. One can find many variations in the embroidery pattern of the eagle's eye, beak, head shape and feathers.

Fig. 101.7. World War II. FE. This variation has an unusual embroidery pattern which produces a ripple effect in the eagle's head.

Fig. 101.8. World War II. FE.

Figs. 101.9 and 101.10. World War II. FE. White tongue variation.

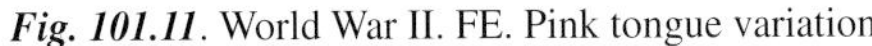

Fig. 101.11. World War II. FE. Pink tongue variation.

Fig. 101.12. World War II. FE with integral numerical designation.

Fig. 101.13. World War II/Post World War II?. FE. Gold eye variation. This patch and *Fig. 101.12* are probably "PX" type patches or ones that were available to a GI to purchase but not issued to him.

Fig. 101.14. World War II/Post World War II? FE. White letter "Airborne" tab variation.

Fig. 101.15. World War II, England. ME on felt.

Fig. 101.16. World War II, England. HE on felt.

Figs. 101.17 and 101.18. World War II, England. Carl Lee. Bullion and sequins on wool.

Figs. 101.19 and 101.20. Post World War II, Germany. FE.

Fig. 101.21. Post World War II, Germany. Lt. Colonel A. Bell. Bullion on felt with HE detail and border.

Fig. 101.22. Post World War II, Germany. HE cello cording on felt with bullion bordered Airborne tab, all on a wool base.

Fig. 101.23. Post World War II, Germany. Bullion on wool with HE details and bullion border. Courtesy of Peter M. Bennethum.

Fig. 101.24. Post World War II, Germany. 101st Airborne Division side of the program for the 84th vs. 101st football game (see ***Fig. 84.28***). No word on who won.

Fig. 102.1. World War II. FE.

Fig. 102.2. Post World War II, TM. ME monogram on an unusual woven background.

Fig. 102.3. Post World War II, Germany. ME on felt.

Fig. 102.4. Post World War II, Germany. HE on felt.

Fig. 102.5. Post World War II, Germany. HE cello cording on felt.

Fig. 102.6. Post World War II, Germany. Bullion on felt with a bullion border.

Fig. 102.7. Post World War II, Germany. Patch type DI with spring pin closure.

Fig. 102.8. Post World War II, Germany. Painted plastic souvenir wall hanging.

Fig. 103.1. Interwar. Felt on felt.

Fig. 103.2. World War II. Three different U.S. made FE patches.

Fig. 103.3. World War II. FE. Yellow border variation.

Fig. 103.4. World War II. Standard FE patch with added dog tag chain border decoration.

Fig. 103.5. Post World War II, Germany. FE.

Fig. 103.6. Post World War II, Germany. HE on wool.

Fig. 103.7. Post World War II, Germany. CS on satin background with applied woven base and ME border.

Fig. 103.8. Post World War II, Germany. HE on felt with bullion detail and border.

Fig. 104.1. Interwar. Felt on felt.

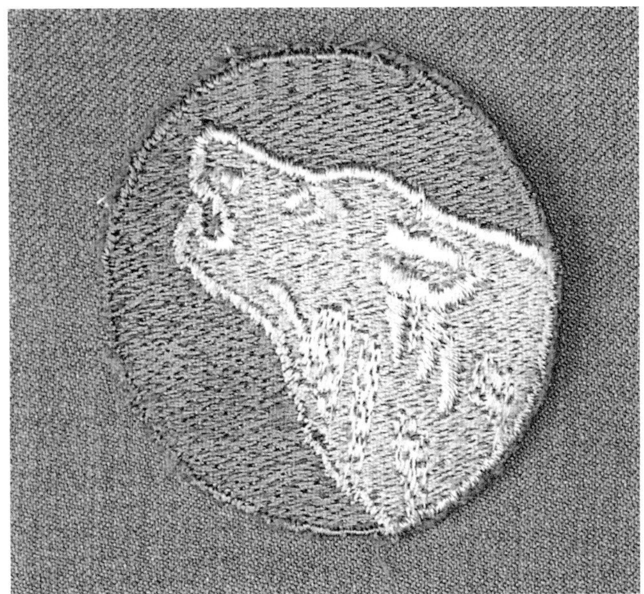

Fig. 104.3. Interwar/World War II. FE.

Fig. 104.2. Interwar. ME on wool.

Fig. 104.4. World War II. FE. Green border variation.

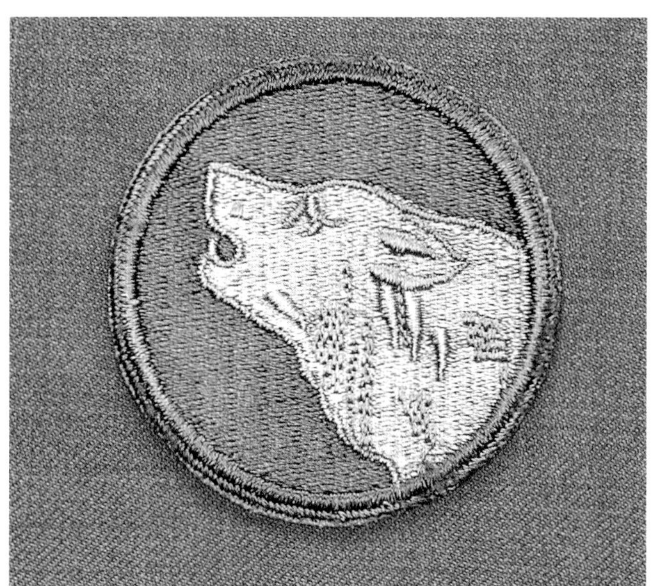

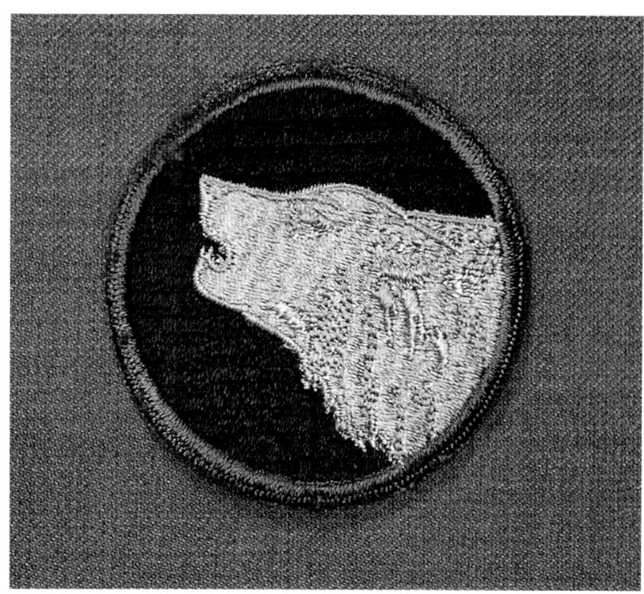

Figs. 104.5 and 104.6. World War II. FE.

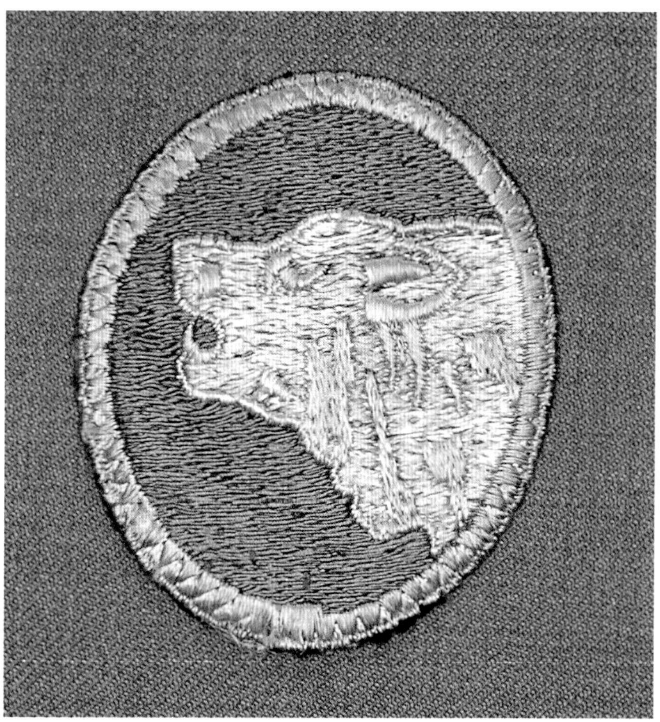

Fig. 104.7. World War II, England. FE.

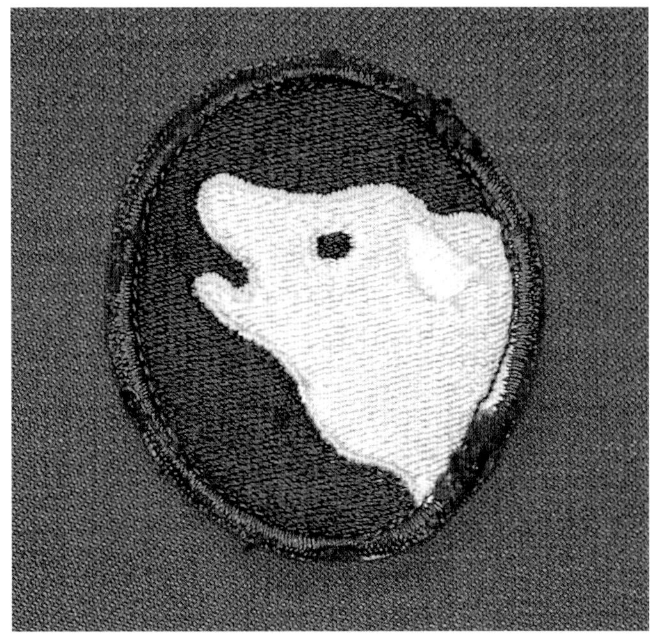

Figs. 104.8 and 104.9. Post World War II, Germany. FE.

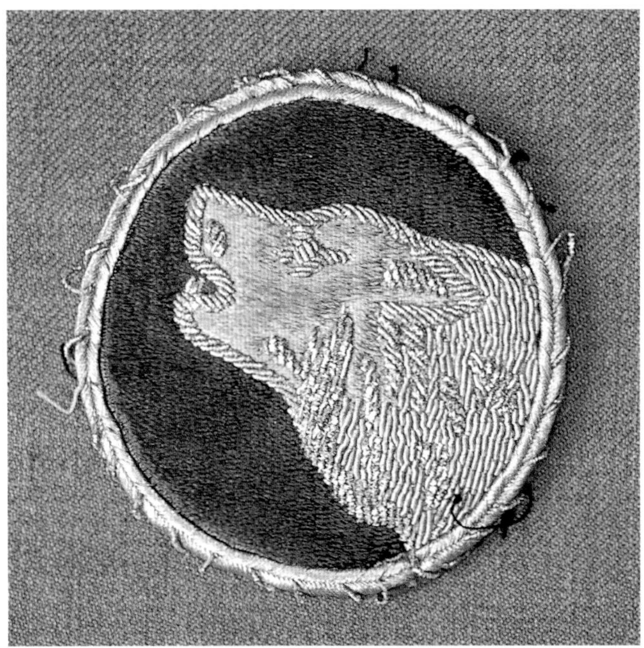

Fig. 104.10. Post World War II. Sgt. David Mendelssohn, 104th Signal Company. U.S. made patch with German added bullion detail and bullion soutache border.

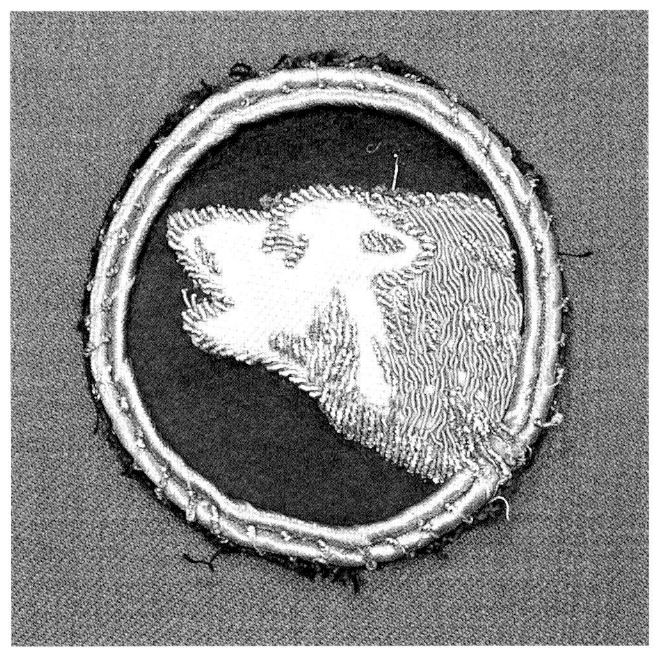

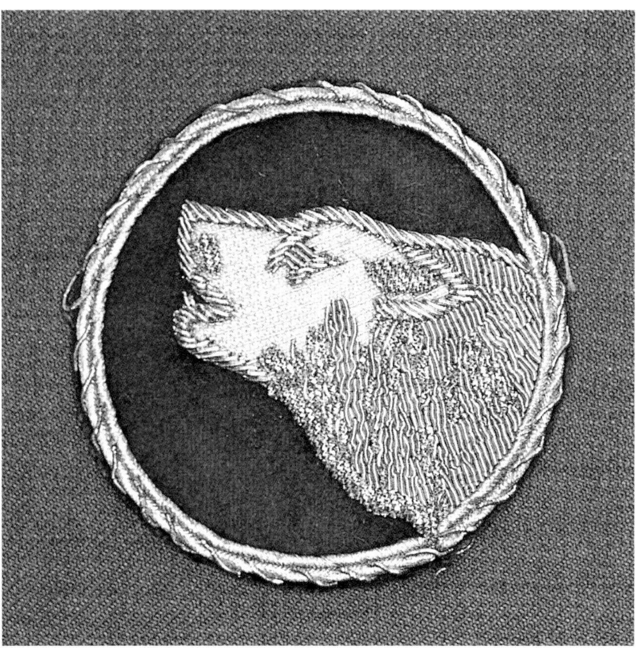

Figs. 104.11 and 104.12. Post World War II, Germany. Bullion on felt with bullion soutache border. ***Fig. 104.12*** is another of Sgt. Mendelssohn's patches.

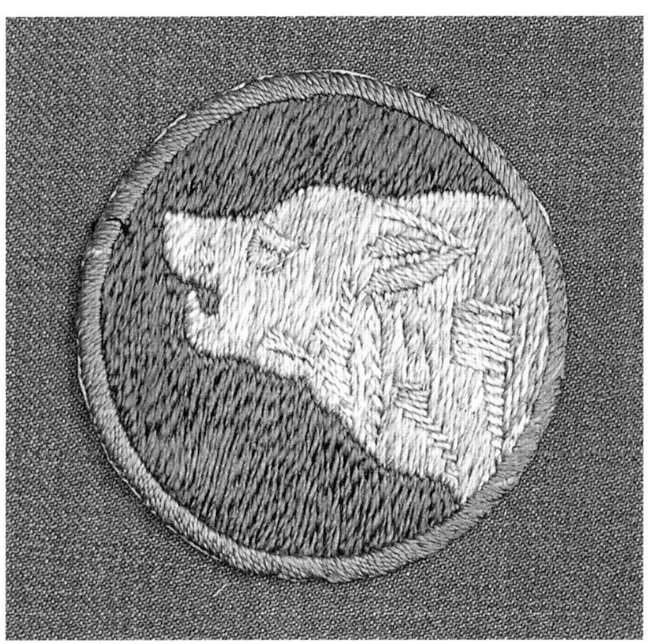

Fig. 104.13. Post World War II, Japan. Fully hand embroidered silk.

Fig. 104.14. World War II. Sgt. Mendelssohn's marskman award with sterling and enamel hand chased 104th Division insignia hanger.

Figs. 106.1 and 106.2. World War II. Four different U.S. made FE patches showing the wide variety of lion head colors and detail differences that can be found.

Fig. 106.3. Post World War II, Germany. FE.

Figs. 106.4 and 106.5. Post World War II, Germany. HE on felt.

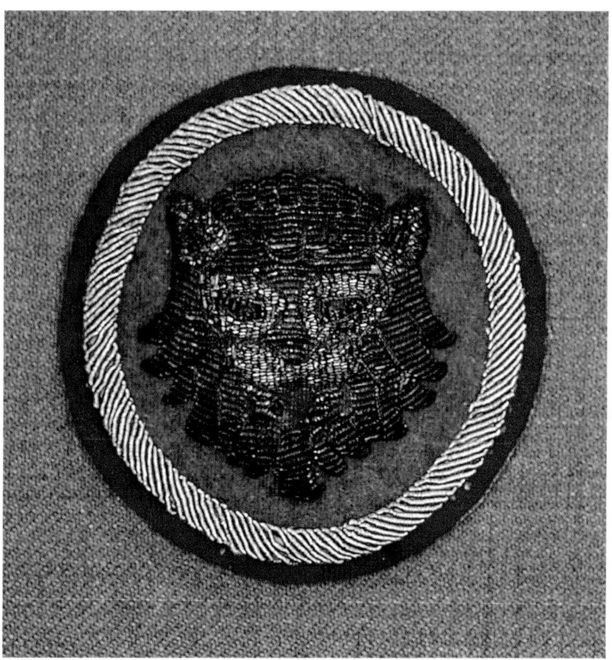

Fig. 106.6. Post World War II, Germany. Bullion on felt with HE details.

Bibliography

Angolia, LTC (Ret.) John R. *Cloth Insignia of the SS*. San Jose, California: R. James Bender Publishing, 1983.

Angolia, John R. and Adolf Schlicht. *Uniforms & Traditions of the German Army 1933-1945 Vol. 1*. San Jose, California: R. James Bender Publishing, 1984.

Britton, Jack and George Washington Jr.. *U.S. Military Shoulder Patches of the United States Armed Forces*. Tulsa, Oklahoma: M.C.N. Press, 1985.

Davis, Martin L. *Insignia of the 42nd Rainbow Division* Rainbow Division Veterans Association, 1985.

Emerson, William K. *Encyclopedia of United States Army Insignia and Uniforms*. Norman: University of Oklahoma Press, 1996.

English, George H., *History of the 89th Division 1917 • 1918 • 1919*, The War Society of the 89th Division, 1920.

Lewis, Kenneth. *Doughboy to GI U.S. Army Clothing and Equipment 1900-1945*. West Midlands, England: Norman D. Landing Publishing, 1993.

Morgan, George O. and Mark Warren. *Shoulder Sleeve Insignia of the A.E.F. 1917-1919*. Keokuk, Iowa: Hill Printing Co., 1986.

Phillips, Stanley S. Civil *War Corps Badges and Other Related Awards, Badges, Medals of the Period*. Lanham, Maryland: S.S. Phillips and Assoc., 1982.

Rottman, Gordon. *U.S. Army Airborne 1940-90*. London, England: Osprey Publishing Ltd., 1990.

Schulz, P.J., H. Otoupalik, and D. Gordon. *World One Collectors Handbook Vols. 1 & 2*. Missoula, Montana: GOS Publishing Inc., 1988.

Smith and Pelz. *Shoulder Sleeve Insignia of the U.S. Armed Forces 1941-1945*. N.p., 1981.

Smith and Pelz. *Shoulder Sleeve Insignia of the U.S. Army 1946 – 1976*. University of Evansville Press, 1978.

Stanton, Shelby. *U.S. Army Uniforms of The Cold War 1948-1973*. Mechanicsburg, Pennsylvania: Stackpole Books, 1994.

Stanton, Shelby. *U.S. Army Uniforms of The Korean War*. Harrisburg, Pennsylvania: Stackpole Books, 1992.

Stanton, Shelby. *U.S. Army Uniforms of World War 2*. Harrisburg, Pennsylvania: Stackpole Books, 1991.

Stanton, Shelby L. *World War II Order of Battle*. New York, New York: Galahad Books, 1984.

Windrow, Martin. *Waffen-SS*. London, England: Osprey Publishing Ltd., 1971.

Author's Note

Would you like to contribute to a revision of this book or other volumes? If so, please contact the authors courtesy of the publisher. The authors are actively seeking contributions in the form of original patches, period pictures and related insignia to photograph. Future titles will also cover the period from World War I through the post Korean War era. The subject areas currently being worked on are: Armor and Cavalry; Armies, Corps and Commands; Artillery, Army Aviation, Engineers, Infantry, Medical, Military Police, Ordnance, Quartermaster, Signal and Special Units (Airborne, Ranger etc.); Army Air Service, Army Air Corps, Army Air Force and Pre-Vietnam Air Force.

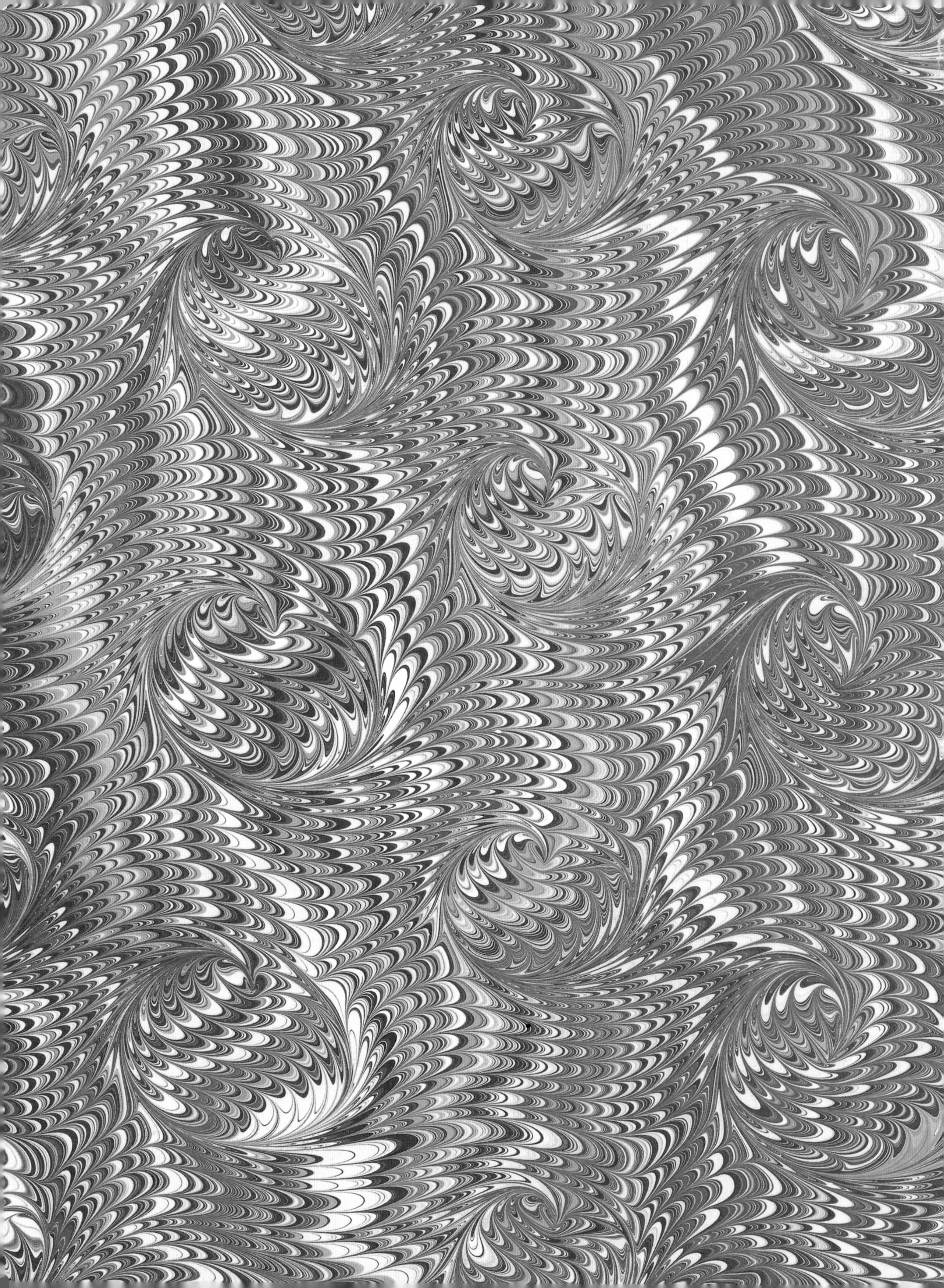